TO: Kirk

on our 13th Anniversary

1999

love Tracey

Guiding
Your
Family

in a
Misguided
World

D0611053

FOCUS ON THE FAMILY.

TONY EVANS

Guiding Your Family

in a Misguided World

TYNDALE

Tyndale House Publishers, Wheaton, Illinois

GUIDING YOUR FAMILY IN A MISGUIDED WORLD

Copyright © 1991 by Dr. Anthony T. Evans

Library of Congress Cataloging-in-Publication Data

Evans, Anthony T.
    Guiding your family in a misguided world / Anthony T. Evans.
        p.   cm.
    Includes bibliographical references.
    ISBN 1-56179-673-5 (pbk.) : $7.95
    1. Child rearing—Religious aspects—Christianity.   2. Child
rearing—United States. I. Title.
HQ769.3.E82   1991
248.8′45—dc20   91-4397
                                                       CIP

A Focus on the Family book published by
Tyndale House Publishers, Wheaton, Illinois.

Unless otherwise noted, Scripture quotations are from the *New American Standard Bible,* © 1960, 1963, 1968, 1971, 1973, 1975 and 1977 by The Lockman Foundation.

People's names and certain details of incidents mentioned in this book have been changed to protect the privacy of the individuals involved.

All rights reserved. International copyright secured. No part of this publication may be reproduced, stored in a retrieval system, or transmitted in any form or by any means—electronic, mechanical, photocopy, recording, or otherwise—without prior permission of the publisher.

Editor: Larry K. Weeden
Designer: Timothy Jones
Cover design: Brad Lind, Candi Park D'Agnese

Printed in the United States of America

99 00 01 02 03 04/10 9 8 7 6 5 4 3 2 1

To my parents and in-laws, Arthur and Evelyn Evans and Basil and Eleen Cannings, for giving my wife and me both physical and spiritual life and teaching us the meaning and importance of family;

to my beloved wife, Lois, for being the most dynamic, faithful, godly wife any man could ask for, and for being the kind of woman our daughters wish to emulate and our sons want to marry;

to my four children, Chrystal, Priscilla, Anthony, Jr., and Jonathan, for the sheer joy and privilege of being your father, and for all the great lessons in parenting you both allowed and forced me to learn and apply;

to my heavenly Father and Savior, the Lord Jesus Christ, "from whom every family in heaven and on earth derives its name" (Eph. 3:15), for including my family in that number.

Contents

Acknowledgments

My sincere thanks go to Mrs. Annie Roberson, my administrative assistant, for her support and encouragement in the development of this book. Thanks also to Mrs. Debbie Anderson for assisting with the transcribing, and to Bill Chickering and Larry Weeden for their helpful insights during the preparation of this project.

Foreword

Like a sand castle on the water's edge in a rising tide, the Christian family stands in a precarious position. What started as a sporadic spray that slowly pocked the walls of family values has now become the crashing waves of mainstream American society.

At one time, we could guard our families simply by avoiding certain T.V. programs, taking our children to Sunday school, and teaching them to avoid those few peers who were part of the "bad" element. When those few peers turned into the majority, we pulled our children into Christian schools, limited T.V. access only to PBS and the Disney channel, and erected higher and higher walls of isolation to keep bad influences from soaking past our defenses.

Today, the waves rise even higher. What was once "safe" T.V. is now full of messages about weak fathers, incompetent mothers, and rebellious children. At one time, a parent's request was met by a "Yes, sir," "Okay," "Uh," or at least an "Oh, all right." Today, we're more likely to get, "Don't have a cow, man!" "Chill out, dude!" Any five-year-old can talk about divorce, ten-year-olds are exposed to drugs, and twelve-year-olds face sexual pressure. Even kids in Christian schools are not immune.

The walls of isolation we have so carefully

constructed are no longer guaranteed to keep out antifamily values and influences. Messages of sexual license, materialism, egotism, and rebellion screaming out the creed of self-advancement at all costs are on our billboards, in our movies, in newspaper ads, in our jobs—and even in our churches.

Do we give up? Do we retreat even further? Is it time to hide our light under a bushel to keep it from being extinguished by the waves of a degenerate society? Or perhaps, with our frigate badly damaged and facing a larger foe asking for our surrender, we answer back like John Paul Jones, "We have not yet begun to fight."

God has provided us with the weapons of prayer, His Word, and His indwelling Holy Spirit. They are far more powerful than anything we face in our world. Many have chosen to fight back through media boycotts, political rallies, and school board protests. Those are important, but they are only as effective as the family structure they're designed to protect. The family is singularly strategic.

As parents, we no longer have the luxury of long-distance warfare—sending the kids to Sunday school and a Christian school and letting the "professionals" do the dirty work. Parents must be intimately involved in hand-to-hand combat, spending more effort at becoming models of Christian health and more time with their children, infecting them with personal exposure to Christian values.

Dr. Tony Evans is uniquely qualified to talk about the new type of combat. When many churches fled to the suburbs, where the culture is outwardly more tolerant of Christian values, Tony renewed his vision for strengthening urban churches and families. The inner-city fight is most severe. The pressures the suburbs are now facing so directly have already been present downtown for years. Tony is not writing out of theory, but out of the experience of a battle-scarred veteran struggling to be God's instrument in saving marriages, healing victims of child abuse, and proclaiming a message of hope in places where hope died long ago. Most importantly, Tony is a father struggling to pass on to his own four children the message of Christ through his personal example so they are prepared to face the onslaught of an anti-Christian world without retreat and without defeat.

Tony is plugged in to the pressures and pitfalls of this generation. Tony also is completely committed to the sufficiency of the Scriptures to address the needs of even the ugliest parts of our world. This is not a book designed to raise your level of comfort. If you would rather not hear about how society is doing everything it can to tear down your family, or if you're already confident you can handle those pressures, I recommend you read no further. However, if you want an accurate, gut-level, no-holds-barred assessment of what you and your family are actually facing and some powerful answers from Scripture on how to protect them and fight back with God's power, I know you will not be disappointed.

Howard G. Hendricks
Chairman, Center for Christian Leadership
Distinguished Professor, Dallas Theological Seminary

CHAPTER ONE

A World That Destroys Families

Kramer vs. Kramer, one of the most highly acclaimed motion pictures of recent years, won Oscars in 1979 for best picture, best director, best actor (Dustin Hoffman), and best supporting actress (Meryl Streep). It also showcased one of the typical attitudes of our misguided world.

Streep and Hoffman played the parts of a wife and husband living in New York City with their young son. Early in the film, the wife announced she'd had enough of their unhappy marriage and was leaving. She promptly took off, forcing the father and son to cope without her and with the pain of her rejection.

Later, however, just when Dad and the boy were beginning to come to terms with Mom's desertion and get on with life, she

1

reappeared and said she wanted custody of their son.

Her explanation for why she left in the first place? "I had to *find myself*," she said, even though her search came at incredibly high cost to her husband and child. And now that she felt good about "who I am" and concluded she wanted to be a mother after all, she expected to just walk back in and take possession of the boy.

That kind of self-centered, hurtful thinking, where "my needs" take priority over everything else, is all too common in our society today. It's part of a culture that is destroying homes by the thousands, including many Christian families, where the selfishness may be more subtle but is no less real.

There are no shortcuts when it comes to building a healthy, loving and caring family. It requires time, tears, hard work, and sacrifice, putting others first. It also requires the ability to recognize the influence of our misguided world on our own families and the wisdom to guide ourselves and our children safely through it according to biblical principles and values.

An Eroding Culture

Can there be any doubt that our society is eroding at a frightening pace? The greatest threat to our nation does not come from any force or power outside our borders. The decay is coming from within, and unless there is a reversal—and I mean a rapid reversal—we're looking straight into a terrifying abyss. That chasm results from the destruction of the family structure and an attitude that says the traditional family is not only to be looked down upon, but even reviled. We are well on the way.

Prior to the 1920s, our society shared a certain God-consciousness. Not everyone was Christian, of course, but people recognized there were absolute standards for human conduct growing out of the Bible, and they knew they had to answer to a higher authority—God—for how faithfully they adhered to those standards. Beginning in Europe and spreading west, however, humanism, and with it evolution, started to take hold. Out went moral absolutes; morality became dependent on the situation of the moment. Out went the truth that people are sinful by nature; in came the idea that humanity evolved from lower life forms without God and was constantly improving, so there was no real need for a Savior.

The decline in our culture caused by this loss of God-consciousness is perhaps most obvious in our most visible mass medium, television. As a professional media observer recently wrote, "When it comes to reinforcing traditional values and standards of morality and decency, TV's judgment is clouded by a hostility to anything that smacks of Judeo-Christian mores.

"All too often, today's traditional nuclear family is portrayed in the crudest terms imaginable: Dad, usually a weak character, belches at the dinner table; Mom, formerly a nurturing presence in the home, reigns as the put-down queen; and the children act bratty and disrespectful—and are proud of it.

"With the success of such TV shows as 'Married ... With Children,' 'Roseanne' and 'The Simpsons,' American family life is being satirized, skewered, ridiculed, mocked and held up for contempt—all for the sake of a few laughs."[1]

That same commentator concluded, "No one can predict how far network television will go in the next decade—what new ground will be broken, what taboos forgotten and what limits stretched. But if the 1990 fall season is any indication of the direction TV is headed, we may be approaching a bold new age of explicit sex, violence, horror and bad taste."[2]

Research studies done a few years ago concluded that the average person sees 9,230 actual or implied sex acts per year on TV. And 81 percent of that sexual activity—94 percent on daytime soap operas—is *extra-marital*. That means an average teenager, watching TV for ten years between, say, the ages of eight and eighteen, would see almost 75,000 acts of illicit sex[3]—and television has only grown worse since those studies were done.

The mind-set of television executives comes across loud and clear in this statement by Howard Stringer, president of the CBS Broadcast Group: "It makes me nervous that more shows don't reach out on a kinkier level or a more dramatic or exotic level."[4]

You may respond, "I don't let my children watch much TV, and I choose their programs carefully." If that's true, you're more diligent than most parents. Research shows that while average American third-graders spend 900 hours per year in the school classroom, they spend 1,170 hours watching television—more than 3 hours per day, each and every day of the year.[5]

Many of you reading this book know your kids come close to that average, or maybe exceed it. *But even if they watch no television, their friends, neighborhood pals, classmates, and church buddies are watching, and they have enormous influence on your children.* In fact, surveys indicate that in the teen years, peers have replaced parents as the number one shaper of values and behavior.[6] There's simply no way to protect our sons and daughters completely from the onslaught of our culture's corrupt values. Even apart from TV programs, the movies, TV and magazine ads, popular music, billboards, t-shirts, and just the things kids talk about (everyone knows Spuds McKenzie is a party animal and that Madonna has made the bra a fashion item) all combine to indoctrinate our children.

And what messages are being hammered into them? *Love is purely physical, it's indiscriminate, it's for the moment only, it's cheap. You've got to get as much as you can right now, because in a few years you're not going to be as attractive anymore, and it will be harder to find the "love" you need. Besides, everyone is doing it. Just do it safely.*

Those messages are aimed at our kids, tomorrow's parents. And though it breaks my heart, I'm not surprised anymore when I hear about a thirteen-year-old girl getting pregnant.

Speaking of the media and popular music, consider the way both manhood and womanhood are reviled in concerts, in TV programs featuring rock music, and in music videos. Our kids see stars such as Bobby Brown pull a woman on stage, lay her on her back, sit on top of her, and grind his hips into her body while he belts out his song. George Michael shows the depth of relationship he's looking for when he sings to teenagers, "I want your sex."

Or our children see "the Artist Formerly Known as Prince" standing on stage surrounded by backup singers wearing skimpy lingerie. One by one, he walks over to each woman and seductively dances with her. Kids can also watch Madonna, naked and chained to a bed, waiting expectantly for a muscular man at her door. They observe famous supermodels sporting barely-there swimsuits and underwear in mainstream magazines and mall-store window posters.

Young people don't need any special equipment to watch this stuff. Any five-year-old who can flip the channels can see it, even without cable.

Psychologist Dr. James Dobson has summarized well the tragedy of the sexual messages bombarding our children: "How sorry I am for the pressures we have allowed to engulf them. How regretful I am of the sexual enticements that reach their ears during elementary school—teaching them that virginity is a curse and sex an adolescent toy."[7]

Besides the encouragement to indulge in premarital sex, our cultural erosion is seen in things like the anti-Christian art we're forced to subsidize with our tax dollars through the grants given by the National Endowment for the Arts (NEA). It's hard to believe that anyone would consider a portrayal of a cross standing in a vial of urine to be art, but that's the level to which our society has fallen.

In a recent Ann Landers advice column, a mother actually wrote and asked if it was okay for her twenty-three-year-old, divorced daughter to parade naked in front of her sixteen-year-old brother. Can you believe that any parent would need to ask such a question? Yet in our society, that mother could easily be your next-door neighbor.

A full-page ad in the October 15, 1990, issue of *Newsweek* magazine promoted "National Coming Out Day," encouraging homosexuals to be more proud and open about their sinful lifestyle. Across the country, the gay rights community is also pushing for laws that would give homosexual couples the same legal status and rights as traditional families—including the right to adopt children.

It doesn't take a prophet to look out the window these days and see where we're heading. Sometimes I wonder just how far down we'll have to go before we wake up.

A Matter of Priorities

Another of our society's sins that has overwhelmed us is materialism. We live in a prosperous nation. Most of us have cars, decent housing, money, and all the creature comforts we could ever need (though never as much as we want). The yuppie mentality and Me Generation's pursuit of more and more has clearly infected us in the church as much as the world around us. And our culture continues to drive home the message that what we are and have already just isn't enough.

Each day, husbands, wives, and children are hit with a barrage of stimuli telling them there is much more to life than raising a family; there's much more to life than nurturing children and providing a solid foundation for the next generation. There are sleek new cars and clothes to buy, credit cards to use, and fine wines to taste.

Those messages all tell us, "What you have isn't the latest fashion. Who you are isn't good enough. You can have more if you want it. In fact, you can have it all." As a nation, we've borrowed and borrowed in pursuit of that lie, leading to the all-too-often-true bumper sticker that says, "I owe, I owe, it's off to work I go."

I got a good dose of materialism combined with peer pressure when Chrystal, my older daughter, was in high school. One day she came home and announced that she *had* to get a car of her own. Why? One of her friends had just received *her* own car, and now Chrystal would be embarrassed to be seen getting on the bus!

When she finally got her driver's license, Lois and I would sometimes let her drive our minivan to school. But did that satisfy her? Not at all. The minivan was "too much like a truck," and it was "embarassing" to be seen driving it.

I told her that if she didn't stop complaining, she would find herself walking, but the point is that all my logical arguments against getting her a car were to no avail. I could not get past the materialistic influence of her friends. (Thankfully, time and maturity have changed her way of thinking.)

We have also been sucked in by shifting morals and values. We now think of divorce as a ready option to commitment, and abortion as an issue of personal freedom rather than one involving life, death, and responsibility before God.

The pace of our society, coupled with the financial pressures that lead to two-career families, has worked steadily to push us toward abdicating much of our parental duty. Millions of our kids are now turned over to child-care workers, day-care centers, and the television. Those children receive much of their teaching and their first impressions of life from people other than their parents. And many of those kids are part of a recent and terrible phenomenon known as "latchkey kids"—young children who come home from school each day to an empty home and no supervision. They turn on the television and get their minds filled with whatever the producers want them to see and hear.

You can read about this destruction of priorities most anywhere, but it struck me hardest in an article that appeared in a recent issue of *Fortune* magazine. The writer's theme was the workaholic tendencies of up-and-coming executives.

One story he told was of a woman who runs a large baking company. It described her six- and sometimes seven-day work week, her sixteen-hour work days, her health club regimen, her glamorous business associates, and how much she pampers her dog. And although you read nothing on this particular topic during the whole story, the last sentence simply says, "She has two young children."

What an indictment! Lest you think, however, that I'm taking off after women with careers, let me throw a very sobering number at you. The average American *father* spends *less than half a minute each day in meaningful conversation* with his children. That boils down to about three hours a year. The husband, the father, the one who should be the spiritual director of the home!

Is there a question anymore about why

our families and our nation are decaying spiritually? Part of the answer is that we fathers never talk to our kids!

When was the last time you saw a television show in which a family went to church together on Sunday? Chances are, you can't remember a last time. In subtle ways like these, and in not-so-subtle ways, our children are told their faith is silly, irrational, unsophisticated, and out of touch. The public schools, under the banner of academic freedom and separation of church and state, convey the same message.

You can't go much lower than to bring down the faith of a child. Yet it happens thousands of times a day in our country. That's why it disturbs me when I see articles, pamphlets, and books on the theme of "What's Gone Wrong with Our Kids?"—as if the problem and the solution rested with them. Our kids are not just a lost generation; they're also the product of a lost generation.

It's not the kids' fault their parents fail to give them unconditional love and lots of attention; it's not kids who ship in the drugs from overseas; it's not kids who produce the shows promoting materialism and telling them sexual promiscuity has no negative consequences; it's not kids brewing the beer and the liquor; and it's not kids producing magazines and films filled with pornography and violence and then setting them out on display at a convenience store.

I want to be clear on this. Our children will learn and become what their parents, their teachers, and their culture impart to them. If we teach them that values are relative, should we really be surprised when they grow up with a distorted sense of right and wrong? If they see film after film in which the hero is a Rambo walking off into the sunset over several hundred corpses, how will they perceive success? When young men are repeatedly shown that the true test of manhood is how many women you can "score" with, and they see more and more Christian leaders caught in sexual sin, why should we be surprised at the yearly rise in teenage pregnancies? Why do we recoil when we read, for example, that in the city of Milwaukee, Wisconsin, over half the births each year are out of wedlock?

Cheapened Life

Our culture has also cheapened life, and by cheapening life, we have cheapened the family. We abort children before they're born, let television baby-sit our kids, and institutionalize people when they get too old and difficult to care for. We're also moving ever closer to legalized euthanasia, and there's serious talk that the elderly should be willing to commit suicide when they're no longer "productive" so as to stop being a "drain" on the earth's resources.

Between those two poles of the cradle and the grave—from the womb to the tomb—are the multitude of social injustices that bear on the quality of life people experience. God requires that people be treated with respect and that the poor and downtrodden, orphans and widows, be assisted and protected. The issue of justice in society is so important to God that He has destroyed whole nations where injustice prevailed. True religion is defined as the presence of justice in society. Yet in our selfish culture, the poor are often despised, locked out of equal access and opportunity, and kept poor by governmental systems that make it more profitable to abandon the family rather than reunite it.

God has some powerful and loving things to say about young and old and those in between. I get angry when I hear an unborn child described only as a fetus or a "product of conception." Then I ponder God's view of the unborn as it's written in Psalm 139:13-15: "It was you who created my inmost self and put me together in my mother's womb; for all these mysteries I thank you: for the wonder of myself, for the wonder of your works.

You know me through and through from having watched my bones take shape when I was being formed in secret, knitted together in the womb."

What the psalmist described is life in all its glory and fullness—not a product, a throwaway, or an inconvenience. God loves and is intimately concerned with each person from the very moment of conception. His will for our lives is known by Him while we're being put together cell by cell.

Concerning the elderly, God said directly to the people of Israel, "Rise in the presence of the aged, show respect for the elderly and revere your God" (Lev. 19:32). And through Solomon He told us, "Listen to your father, who gave you life, and do not despise your mother when she is old" (Prov. 23:22). There is no room for disrespectful treatment of the elderly or euthanasia in God's Word.

A Realistic Hope

By now it should be clear that ours is not a Christian culture. In fact, in many ways it is openly antagonistic toward biblical values and lifestyle. That's ironic, because in a recent Gallup poll, three of every four Americans claimed to have made a personal commitment to Jesus Christ as their Savior—if true, that would be more than 180 million people.

Regardless of its real size, however, I believe with all my heart that the church of Jesus Christ is the strongest force for positive change on this planet. My Bible tells me that just a handful of Christians can make a big difference. Two thousand years ago, twelve of them turned the world upside down. I believe that can happen again; our culture can still be turned around before it's too late. (If you'd like to explore in more depth the role of the church in transforming society, please read my book *America's Only Hope*.)

Whatever our culture's condition, however, there are practical steps we can take as parents and spouses to guide our own families through this misguided world. Those steps are the focus of the rest of this book.

My wife, Lois, and I have four wonderful children: Chrystal; Priscilla; Tony, Jr.; and Jonathan. And like concerned parents everywhere, we want our kids to grow into mature Christian people whose faith is strong, whose desire is to serve and please the Lord, and who know how to tell right from wrong and truth from error. So please understand that even as you prayerfully work to put this book's principles into action in your own family, we're doing the same right alongside you.

Guiding our families through this misguided world has to begin with a realization and an acceptance of the fact that we do live in a misguided world—a world that's working against our purpose as Christian parents. We're in the middle of what Dr. Dobson rightly identifies as a civil war of values, with our children as the prize to the winner. Bringing that truth home has been the goal of this chapter.

We must rise from our beds of complacency. We must not assume someone else will take care of our families, and we must not get caught up in petty concerns—what Campus Crusade for Christ president Bill Bright so aptly calls "straightening pictures on the wall of a burning building."

Guiding our families is a big job, and big jobs are handled bit by bit until they're completed. The steps I offer to you in the rest of this book are the ones I've put together during my years of counseling and ministry. They're also a reflection of the joys and struggles I've shared with my own family as we've worked toward becoming a home where the Lord is faithfully served.

As we let Jesus Christ lead us through those steps, let's remember that we have His friendship and His strength to call upon always. Let us pray, listen, wait, and work. The Lord will sustain us.

CHAPTER TWO

The Purpose
of Family

As part of my pastoral ministry, I have had the privilege of serving as chaplain for the Dallas Mavericks of the National Basketball Association. One day when star forward Mark Aguirre was still on that team, he and I played a little one-on-one.

You have to understand that when I'm fooling around with a basketball by myself, I'm fantastic! I can handle the ball like Magic Johnson. I can swish home a shot from anywhere on the court like Michael Jordan. If an NBA scout saw me when I'm having fun like that, I'd be signed to a free-agent contract on the spot.

Playing against Mark Aguirre, however, was a totally different story. Suddenly, I didn't look like an all-star anymore. My ball-handling was quickly revealed to be more like that of a butcher than that of a top point guard. And in the face of opposition from six feet, six inches of true basketball talent, my shooting was more like that of a bricklayer than that of a premier three-point scorer.

Whenever I remember that lesson in humility, I also remember Philippians 4:13, which says, "I can do all things through Him who strengthens me." Unfortunately for me on the day I went up against Mark Aguirre, that verse doesn't mean I can instantly become an athletic giant at my convenience (as much as I might have wished it did!). God clearly never intended for me to play in the NBA.

What the verse does mean is that the Lord will give us the strength to do everything He has commanded us to do. He doesn't want us to be defeated and frustrated. His will, which includes guiding our families through a misguided world, is challenging and sometimes impossible in our own strength, but we can do it all as we abide in Him and draw on His strength (see John 15:4-5).

Suppose the star player on an NBA team went over to the bench in the middle of a game and whined to the coach because every time he tried to take a shot, the other team put their hands in his face and made it hard to see the basket. Suppose he also complained that every time he tried to dribble the ball, an opponent tried to steal it, making the star so frustrated he couldn't cope.

No coach would stand for such a display of weakness. Why? Because the star is being paid millions of dollars to do exactly what he's complaining about: score consistently in spite of tough opposition. That's his job. That's the special ability for which he receives the big bucks.

Similarly, we Christian parents can dunk the ball of effective family life in spite of the secularism that seeks to block us. Sure it's hard to raise kids today. Sure our culture doesn't support our values the way it used to. Sure it's tough to make ends meet. But we can prevail over the opposition anyway, because we're "million dollar superstars," since greater is He who is in us than he who is in the world (see 1 John 4:4).

Successfully guiding our families has to start, however, with knowing just what God's will is. From His perspective, what's the purpose of the family? What should be our goals as parents? We need to know these things and keep them in mind as we go on in later chapters to consider how best to direct our families. We need to see the "big picture" so we'll understand how all the pieces fit together to complete it.

Spreading His Image

As I study the Bible, I find three reasons why God created marriage and family. The first is what we might call procreation with a purpose. God told Adam and Eve in Genesis 1:28 to "be fruitful and multiply, and fill the earth." Think about it. Eve was the only woman around, and Adam was the only man, and God told them (which I'm sure they didn't mind!) to populate the whole earth.

What He meant was that they should have plenty of babies—so many babies that by the time they were through, their children would be all over the earth. Why? The verse goes on to say, "and subdue it [the earth]; and rule…"

The purpose for having babies is not simply to make look-alikes of yourself. From God's perspective, the reason is for the one creature made in God's image to take dominion over the world. In other words, God wanted Adam and Eve to fill the world so that wherever you walk on planet earth, His image would be there. The mark of God is upon us (even though it was badly tarnished in the Fall). "And God created man in His own image, in the image of God He created him; male and female He created them" (Gen. 1:27).

God wants and enables us to have children because He wants the mark of God to be transferred. If we have children and are not exercising biblical dominion—that is, conveying the mark of God from our generation to our children—we negate the whole purpose of having kids.

I have four children. If I do my job and one of my children moves to Los Angeles, the image of God will be in Los Angeles, on the block where that child lives. If one of my kids goes to Seattle, the image of God will be in Seattle. If one moves to New York, the image of God will now be transferred there. If one goes to Miami, God will be represented there. Thus, God will cover the four corners of the country. The failure to raise children for this reason is to fail in our primary role as parents.

This reason for family puts our parental assignment to raise our kids in the nurture and admonition of the Lord in a very serious light. It's important to God, and therefore to us, that we be intentional about how we train our children, especially in light of the way our culture would mislead them.

Completion

A second reason for marriage and family is our completion. The Lord said to Adam, "I will make you a helpmate who will respond to you, who will assist you" (Gen. 2:18, my paraphrase). To put it another way, God gave us marriage because once God is ready for us to be married, we find ourselves somehow to be less than we were meant to be until we get the help of a mate. (I recognize the Lord calls some folks to a healthy lifetime of singleness [see 1 Cor. 7:1-7], but His plan for most is marriage.) God gave Adam somebody who would complete him, a person distinct from him who would make up what he lacked.

Many people say, "My spouse and I are so different," as if that's a major problem. But what do we expect? If both partners were the same, one would be unnecessary. The whole point of being different is that each person has what the other doesn't have, desperately needs, and can't progress without. One spouse is outgoing, while the other is shy. Perfect! The outgoing person needs to be more subdued, and the shy person needs to be a little outgoing. They can help each other. That's why God brought them together.

Illustrating the Divine

The third reason for marriage and family is divine illustration: to provide a model on earth of our marriage with Christ in heaven. There's no marriage as we know it in heaven,

Jesus told us in Mark 12:25 (some of you are saying, "Thank God!"), and that's because the illustration is no longer needed when you have the real thing.

In Ephesians 5, Paul explained the relationship between husband and wife as being parallel to Christ's relationship with the church. He commanded husbands, for example, to "love your wives, just as Christ also loved the church" (v. 25). Paul went on to issue other well-known commands to husbands and wives, and then he concluded the passage with the following statement: "This mystery is great, but I am speaking with reference to Christ and the church" (v. 32).

Paul was saying, in effect, "If you thought I was talking about husbands and wives, you missed the point." That's why, if our marriages are bad—especially as believers—we're giving the world a bad illustration of Christ and the church. And that's a serious concern to the Father.

Marriage and family are also meant to illustrate the Trinity. What is the Trinity? Three powerful persons who are distinct and yet one entity. They share the same essence—the same divinity, power, holiness, eternal existence without beginning or end, and so on. Yet they are distinct: the Spirit is not the Father, the Father is not the Son, the Son is not the Spirit.

In a similar way, husbands and wives share the same human essence. Both are made from the same clay that God created, and both are made in His image, exhibiting many of His traits (e.g., personality, will, emotions). When those two come together, out of their relationship is born another who is different from either of them, yet has the essence of both. The three people in the family share an essential oneness, yet they're still distinctive persons.

That's how mother, father, and child illustrate the unique unity and diversity that exist in God Himself. This earthly picture of the Trinity is another of God's divine purposes for the family.

The Covenant of Marriage

We've looked now at three of God's purposes for marriage and family. The understanding they provide is essential to guiding our families in a misguided world. (I daresay you haven't seen secular television offer that perspective on family.) But we also need to be reminded of how God views the marriage relationship. His will is the compass by which we steer.

According to the Bible, marriage is a covenant. Malachi 2:14 says, "The Lord has been a witness between you and the wife of your youth, against whom you have dealt treacherously, though she is your companion and your wife by covenant."

What is a covenant? It's similar to a contract, yet different in one significant way. Both are legally binding agreements between two or more parties. If one party does not fulfill its contractual responsibilities, a court can be called upon to enforce the agreement by imposing the specified penalties.

There's one critical part of a covenant that isn't necessarily true of a contract, however. Namely, a covenant is based on a personal relationship. In contracts, no personal relationship is required—only a legally binding agreement. But covenants are *predicated* on relationships.

A biblical covenant is a divinely established, legally binding relationship between two or more parties who agree to function under a designated structure of authority in accordance with revealed guidelines, resulting in long-term consequences. Let's analyze this definition as it applies to the marriage covenant.

First, covenants are legally binding relationships established by God. That is, God is in charge because He created the people who make up the marriage relationship, and He created the relationship itself.

Most couples symbolically include God

in the wedding ceremony by using a preacher, having scriptures read, reciting God's name as part of the vows, and having their wedding performed in the church. God is usually left standing at the altar, however, while the couples build their families without Him. God expects to be a functional part of all aspects of the marriage and family relationship. He isn't interested in a courtesy nod; He wants to run the whole show.

A family's ability to overcome the world's destructive pressure is directly related to the position of authority Christ has in the household. Satan understood this, and that's why he challenged God's authority in the garden with Adam and Eve. He knew that if they became their own gods, setting their own agenda, their family would be destroyed.

The marriage covenant is also legally binding. That's why we have documentation related to the relationship (the marriage license), and it's also why there must be a legal decree before we can get out of it. There's nothing casual about marital responsibility. The covenant obligates us to the welfare of others under God.

In this day of me-ism, no-fault divorces, and live-in relationships, people have lost the seriousness of marriage. Consequently, many couples want to hedge their marital bets by signing prenuptial agreements. They're looking for an easy escape hatch without any inconvenience.

A little girl once noticed how big and cumbersome her grandmother's wedding band was. "Grandmother," she asked, "how come your ring is so thick?"

"Because in my day they were made to last," the woman said.

That's the way God meant for marriage to be—solid, binding, enduring.

The parties involved in a covenant also agree to function under a designated structure of authority. That is, they agree to function in their God-ordained roles.

God's blessings come to us through a specific chain of command. First Corinthians 11:3 says that God the Father is over Christ, Christ is over every man, and the man is over his wife. The concern here is not equality of essence. Just as Jesus is equal to God the Father, so women are equal to men. As we read in Galatians 3:28, "There is neither Jew nor Greek, there is neither slave nor free man, *there is neither male nor female; for you are all one in Christ Jesus*" (emphasis added). But Paul, who wrote both passages under the inspiration of the Holy Spirit, was talking about a distinction in function.

The moment anyone leaves his or her God-given role, chaos sets in. If Christ the

Son had wanted to be the Father, nobody would have been saved. People living independent of Christ's direction over their lives make up their own rules of what maleness and femaleness are all about, which brings disaster to the home and the culture.

New and bizarre definitions of manhood have led to massive numbers of homosexual men; brutal, wife-beating men; insensitive, uncaring men; and passive, irresponsible men. This corruption explains why we have a women's liberation movement—it started and grew as it did because of bad male leadership.

No sane woman wants to be delivered from somebody who loves her twenty-four hours a day, embracing, complimenting, and encouraging her. Generally speaking, women will gladly be submissive to that kind of man. The anticipation of such love is what makes women want to get married in the first place. It's only after the wedding that they want to be free.

Women have a role to play, too, and that's to submit properly to the authority of their husbands so that God's blessing can flow from him to her and from her to the children. Women who disrespect their men hinder the free flow of God's grace through the home. That's why Paul told wives who have unbelieving husbands to remain in the home if at all possible—so their presence can be the channel God uses to provide His grace and protection to the husband and children (see 1 Cor. 7:14).

Children must also function in their proper role of honoring their parents if they wish to have a good quality of life and enjoy their full allotment of days (see Eph. 6:2-3). They, like all family members, must obey those above them, and all must obey God if they're going to experience His blessing.

Satan understood this principle as well, which explains why, in the Garden of Eden, he tempted Eve first. He got the man and woman to reverse their roles. She became the leader, the principal decision maker. Adam became the passive male standing on the sidelines, listening to that sneaky snake lure his wife away from his leadership and God's Word and into his own program for the family.

The next element of a covenant is that people agree to function in accordance with revealed guidelines. That is, God sets the rules.

The world, however, has set up different rules, and we're dancing to its tune. God says virginity until marriage is a virtue; the world says there is nothing wrong with premarital sex. God says parents are responsible for the welfare of their children; the world says the state is responsible. God says corporal punishment is an important part of discipline; the world says it produces insecurity in children.

The issue for the Christian family is who will be obeyed? In their wedding vows, couples end their oaths with "so help me God." But from then on, they march to their own drumbeat.

Again, this is where Satan attacked our first parents. By raising the question "Hath God said?" he was challenging God's rule book. He was saying, "I have a new set of rules; listen to me." They listened to him and disobeyed God. They got to do their own thing and paid dearly for it, which leads to the final element of a covenant.

A covenant has long-term consequences. The deterioration of our culture morally and spiritually is no fluke. We're paying the price in our children for the failure of their parents to function in accordance with God's ordained purpose and plan for family life. When Adam and Eve rebelled against God, Cain wound up killing Abel. We're still feeling the death blow of their deed in the ongoing sinfulness of humanity.

We have only just begun to see the devastation that will take place across America as this generation of children begins to have its own kids and passes on the legacy of rebellion. God's Word is fulfilling itself as these rebels are producing a terrible loss in the quality of life we used to enjoy.

A Biblical Picture

In Psalm 128, God provided a word picture that shows us what a family looks like when it operates God's way—when it knows God's purpose and abides by the laws of a covenant. We read in verse 1, "How blessed is everyone who fears the Lord, who walks in His ways."

The Hebrew word for *blessed* there means "internal happiness." If we want happiness, we have to begin with our relationship to God. Money, possessions, fame—none of these things, and not even working to make a good marriage, will give us real, lasting happiness if we don't fear the Lord and walk with Him in obedience day by day and moment by moment.

Why are there a lot of unhappy marriages and families? Because there are a lot of unhappy people in them, people who aren't walking close to the Lord. You've either got happiness or you don't; it's a by-product of a right relationship with Him, not something you can buy.

To fear God means several things. First, it means we take Him seriously—as folks say in everyday language, "as serious as a heart attack." We don't just nod our heads during a Sunday sermon and live the other six days of the week as if we hadn't heard a word of the message. When the Bible tells me as a parent to "bring them [my children] up in the discipline and instruction of the Lord" (Eph. 6:4), I realize God will hold me accountable for how well I've done that, so I make specific plans to teach my kids. I don't leave the job to others.

Second, fearing God means looking up to Him in awe and respect. I can relate to that as I think of my own father. I've always held him in high regard because the man is worthy of respect. Ever since he became a Christian at the age of thirty, he has lived in such a way that I cannot find fault with him. I literally have never seen my father sin since that time. I know he sins because he's human, but he has carried himself before me in such a way that I can't help but look up to him and tell people proudly, "That's my dad."

If we can have that kind of admiration for the best of earthly fathers, all of whom are far from perfect, how much more should we respect our heavenly Father?

Third, fearing God means acknowledging He has the right to judge sin and will discipline us in order to correct us. We read in Hebrews 12:9-10, "Furthermore, we had earthly fathers to discipline us, and we respected them; shall we not much rather be subject to the Father of spirits, and live? For they disciplined us for a short time as seemed best to them, but He disciplines us for our good, that we may share His holiness."

Again, I can easily relate to that passage because of my own father. In one of his dresser drawers, he kept a heavy leather razor strap. I dreaded (as did my siblings) the occasional news that I was going to have a "session," as he called it, with him and that strap. I earned those sessions by rebelling against his rules. He was patient, and I'd get several warnings, but there would come the time after constant disobedience when he would say those horrible words: "Meet me in the cellar."

That meant I had to go down to the cellar, strip to my shorts, and wait. Dad wouldn't come down right away; he wanted me to think about what I had done and what the consequences were going to be. Then he would walk down slowly—each step seemed to take an hour. Holding the razor strap, he would stare me in the face and say calmly, "Now, Son, you remember I told you not to do this." Next he'd ask, "Is this ever going to happen again, Son?"

"No, Dad, no," I'd say. "Never again!"

"But Son, are you sure?" he'd ask.

"Dad, you don't know how positive I am

that this is never going to happen again," I'd tell him.

"Okay, Son," he'd say to me, "what I want you to do is come put your head between my knees." (Are you picturing the posture that put me in?)

He would hit me only three times across the seat with that strap, but he hit hard. I learned how to shout when he brought it down. I don't remember ever getting a second session for the same offense, however.

My father lived in such a way that I should have obeyed him just because he told me to. But every now and then, when I disobeyed, his discipline forced me to respect him. God also will discipline us when He can't get our attention and respect any other way, for our good and the good of our families.

Turning back to Psalm 128, we read in verse 2, "When you shall eat of the fruit of your hands, you will be happy and it will be well with you." The sense of the verse is that if you fear God (v. 1), you'll be a relaxed person in a relaxed state of mind. You'll be enjoying life under God.

We live in a hectic, dog-eat-dog world where Dad and often Mom as well are trying to make it. Couples used to scrape by, barely able to afford the rent on that first apartment, yet they were happy. Hot dogs and baked beans were a diner's delight. Do you remember those days? Now couples own three- and four-bedroom homes and eat steak and potatoes, and their families are falling apart.

Why is that the case? As a culture, we've lost the ability to enjoy the fruit of our labor. We've brought the frantic pace and the mess at work into the home. Too often, our children and family-building get the leftovers of our time and energy.

The fear of the Lord, however, gives us back the ability to enjoy life, because "it will be well with you." Hell can't stop what God has planned for us when we walk in His ways. That takes the pressure off—God will take care of us. "Don't break your neck to make it to the top," He says. "Break your neck to know Me, and let Me lift you to the top." As the apostle Peter put it, "Humble yourselves, therefore, under the mighty hand of God, that He may exalt you at the proper time" (1 Pet. 5:6).

Does that mean we don't have to work hard? No. Does it mean we shouldn't try to better ourselves? Of course not. But it does mean we don't have to sell out our families to succeed. If we fear Him—if we take seriously our biblical responsibilities as parents and give them the time and effort they require—He will take care of us, and we can relax.

Fruitful Plants

Finally, we read in Psalm 128:3, "Your wife shall be like a fruitful vine, within your house, your children like olive plants around your table." That verse speaks to the responsibility of husbands for the atmosphere in the home. *If* men are living according to verses 1-2, *then* their wives and children will be like fruitful plants.

A vine grew up the side of a house Lois and I used to own. The next owner tore it all down because it was such a nuisance, but we put up with it because it was beautiful. It would grow in through holes in the window frames and cracks in the brick. It grew so fast that it drove me crazy with the constant need for pruning.

The vine grew fast only in warm weather, however. In winter it just sort of hung there, dormant. The key was having the right atmosphere to produce growth. In the same way, the husband and father creates the atmosphere in the home, and it's his job to make it conducive to the family's growth. He can't bring home a winter attitude and expect a spring's budding and blossoming.

In other words, the man comes home to give, not to get. He seeks to serve his family, even when he's tired and hungry and has had a rough day at work. I quoted the first part of Ephesians 5:25 earlier; now let's pay special attention to the second part: "Husbands, love your wives, just as Christ also loved the church *and gave Himself up for her*" (emphasis added). That giving needs to take place every day, in ways small as well as big, and not just in rare heroic moments. If the wife also works outside the home, there's all the more reason for the man to help with the dishes and laundry, help get the kids ready for bed, and so on.

Sound difficult? It's humanly *impossible* to do it consistently. But then, we're not talking about what we can do on our own.

Under those growth-inducing conditions, a wife will be a fruitful vine, producing luscious grapes that become heart-gladdening, intoxicating wine.

And what of the children ("olive plants around your table")? Again depending on the conditions in which they're raised, they have tremendous potential. They're not full-grown trees yet; they have to be nurtured. But a mature olive tree produces many olives, and their oil is used for healing, for cooking, and for a soothing massage ointment, among other things. Much good for the whole community comes from a well-tended olive tree.

What children need most from their parents are time and attention. No substitutes can replace them or make kids feel loved.

In a recent article titled "Shameful Bequests to the Next Generation," *Time* magazine reported, "Parents who do not spend time with their children often spend money instead. 'We supply kids with things in the absence of family,' says Barbara MacPhee, a school administrator in New Orleans. 'We used to build dreams for them, but now we buy them Nintendo toys and Reebok sneakers.'"

The article goes on to say, "In the absence of parental guidance and affirmation, children are left to soak in whatever example their environment sets. A childhood spent in a shopping mall raises consumerism to a varsity sport; time spent in front of a television requires no more imagination than it takes to change channels.

"'Kids are left alone a lot to cope,' she [a clinical social worker] says, 'and they sense less support from their families.'"[1]

We Christians dare not assume that those facts apply only to the secular family. We need to examine our own priorities and practices. Are we asking our children to raise themselves? Are we letting the TV, neighborhood kids, day-care workers, or the secular school system raise them? Are we too busy or too tired to see that our kids grow into fruitful olive trees instead of weeds?

Psalm 128:4-5 again promises a blessing,

this time "from Zion," to those who fear the Lord. That doesn't mean we'll have big bank accounts. I could introduce you to lots of rich folks who know they're not blessed because their families are torn apart or their children are hooked on alcohol or other drugs.

No, being blessed means having a unified, happy family. It means being able to stand up in church—in Zion, the place where people go to worship God—and testify that He has given you a million-dollar spouse and million-dollar kids who know Him, love Him, and love, serve, and encourage one another.

I was raised in inner-city Baltimore. My parents didn't have much in the way of material possessions. But we did have each other, a meaningful existence, loving relationships, a sense of dignity, and a deep faith in God. Based on the time and attention my folks gave us kids, there was never any reason to doubt their care. Today, however, we have a generation of teenagers who generate upwards of $55 billion annually but still can't buy enough toys to make them forget the sense of alienation and loss of meaning that have become the tragic hallmarks of American family life.

Only by living in our marriages and families as God intended will we be able to guide our loved ones through this misguided world and experience the delight of family life that He wanted for us when He created the institution in the first place.

CHAPTER THREE

The Family's Foundation: Love

One Christmas I got a bicycle for my son Anthony, Jr. To save a little money, I bought it unassembled. When the time came to put it together, I pulled out all the parts and spread them in front of me.

Now, I hate reading directions. *I have a doctorate,* I thought. *I should be able to put a bike together.* Eight hours later, I had only the handlebars on. My wife looked at my futile efforts and gave me a very loving but firm suggestion. "Honey," she said, "why don't you read the directions?"

With my pride whipped, I took her advice, and in two hours the bike was completely assembled.

My work took much longer than necessary because I failed to understand a key point: The maker of the bike knew more about putting it together than I did. When I finally followed the manufacturer's guidelines, I saved myself time, irritation, and stress, and Tony, Jr., had a bicycle that worked.

Unfortunately, when it comes to the spiritual care and feeding of our families, we often go about it the way I tried to assemble my son's bike. We proceed on our own, making things up as we go along, ignoring the clear plans provided by the One who divinely instituted the family.

The family was God's idea. He created it, and if we understand and accept that, we can live under His guidelines and enjoy our families, avoiding a lot of frustration and pain in the process. God knew what He was doing when He put the family together.

But we're stubborn, and we often think we know how to put things together better than God. We think we're smarter than the Designer. We're not.

Love Is God's Idea

Love is also God's idea, and it's the most fundamental foundation of the family. If we're to guide our families safely through a misguided world, we have to lay this part of the foundation carefully and securely. Anything built on a weak foundation will come crashing down sooner or later, and many beautiful-looking homes are falling apart today. They were built on the world's pathetic definition of love, which is nothing more than a temporary feeling at best and a euphemism for sex without commitment at worst (witness the TV soap operas, both day-time and evening).

How do we build our families on true, lasting love? The Manufacturer provided some practical directions in a familiar passage of Scripture.

First Corinthians 13 is commonly called "the love chapter." Although its message is usually discussed in terms of personal growth, its portrait of love applies just as well to the family. What does the apostle Paul have to say about the family? How are we to practice love behind the walls of our homes?

The opening verse of the chapter hits me, as a husband and father, right in the heart: "If I have all the eloquence of men or of angels, but speak without love, I am simply a gong booming or a cymbal clanging."

My biblical role in the family is a position of leadership. As such, I'm often the one doing the talking. And at least when my children were little, they hung on my every word as if God Himself were speaking. Daddy knew it all, or so they thought. It can be exhilarating.

Our work may sometimes put us in similar positions. Perhaps we're making a presentation to an important group, and we've done our preparation and everything flows smoothly. Or maybe we're leading a meeting, and everyone is responsive and the business gets done, to the satisfaction of all, ahead of schedule.

As a preacher, I occasionally feel as though I'm really "on"; the congregation is hanging on every word, and I can't go more than two or three sentences without hearing a chorus of Amens.

Whatever the context in which we feel eloquent and effective in our speech, 1 Corinthians 13:1 says our words ring hollow unless they're backed up by genuine love. While congregations, clients, Sunday school classes, coworkers, and children may hear the voice of an angel, God hears an out-of-tune ego that sounds like an old gong or an irritating and crashing cymbal that won't stop making noise.

When I get home after preaching a sermon that's gone over well, for example, my pride expects to get the same strokes I received at the church. What I sometimes get instead, however, are a lot of those looks that say, "It might be nice if you practiced more of what you preach."

The ability to sound good, to be a leader,

means nothing if it's not matched with a truly loving heart and life.

"If I have the gift of prophecy, understanding all the mysteries there are, and knowing everything, and if I have faith in all its fullness, to move mountains, but am without love, then I am nothing at all" (v. 2).

It's possible to look, act, and even *sound* very spiritual and still amount to nothing. It's possible to be blessed with many gifts of the Spirit and still be bankrupt. Fathers, listen closely: It's possible to be a great spiritual teacher and leader in your family. You know all the verses, understand the principles of the faith, and comprehend the proper teaching and discipline to impart to your children. But if you're out hustling for the extra money and are rarely home; if your idea of submission in marriage is to have your wife awaiting your next command; if your idea of discipline is spanking your children one day for a wrong they've done and letting them get away with it the next day; then Paul says your gifts are built on a foundation other than love, and they are nothing.

Mothers, this goes for you as well. If you treat your husband with disrespect, belittle him in front of your children and others, or fail to open your home in gestures of hospitality and friendship, Paul is telling you that it doesn't matter one iota how many church committees you're on or how many luncheons you attend. It doesn't even matter whether others in the church look to you as a paragon of faith. The foundation for your spiritual appearance is something other than love and in God's eyes is "nothing at all."

"Love is always patient and kind" (v. 4a). The essence of a good teacher is patience, and as parents, we're teachers. Our children are the students. Yet we usually have a harder time being patient with our own kids than we do with others'. When our children attempt a task for the first time and make a mistake, for example, our tendency is to run over, butt in, and take charge. The best thing to do at such a moment is to let them make the mistake, then explain how to do it right the next time. Sometimes the most loving thing we can do is to let go, even if we cringe while doing it.

"Love is never jealous; love is never boastful or conceited; it is never rude or selfish; it does not take offense, and is not resentful" (vv. 4b-5).

Jealousy, pride, and conceit—three deadly enemies of family unity and health. Family members who love one another will encourage each others' talents and gifts. They will not seek to "one-up" each other all the time. Parents, watch this one! I've seen a number of you encourage the talents of one child at the expense of another. Even worse, I've seen parents devalue the gifts of one child with the line, "Why can't you be more like your sister and brother? Look what they can do."

Remember, even if your children's gifts or talents are not the ones you would have chosen for them, they are the gifts and talents God has chosen. Don't let your conceit or your pride get in the way of encouragement. If you and your spouse both graduated from college, for instance, and want your kids to do the same, you're likely to get upset if they want to go to a vocational school and pursue a trade. Your responsibility is to encourage and support them in their choice, not to wish they were more like you.

My goal early in life was to play professional football—a dream that didn't come true. So what did I do? I tried to live out my vision through my older son, Anthony. From the day of his birth, he was surrounded by footballs. He had a football waiting in his crib when he came home from the hospital.

Can you guess how all my efforts to indoctrinate him turned out? Yes, he *hates* football, and the more I bring it up, the more he hates it.

I wanted him to play for me, not for his own enjoyment, and I was loving me and not him. I was raising him in the way I wanted him to go, not in the way he *should go,* which is what Proverbs advises (see 22:6). True love is seeking God's will for the other person, not seeking *your* will *through* your spouse or children.

Love is not a loud and swaggering parent boasting, "Of course we love you. Look at this house. Look at your clothes. Look at what we've given you. How many other kids have this much?"

Love is quiet. It's a thoughtful deed done for your spouse or children with no expectation of return. It's going the extra mile with them, even when you may be too tired to do it.

Love is never rude or selfish. Why is it that we're often gentle and courteous with business associates, friends, and even complete strangers, yet for some reason we don't feel the need to extend any of this to our own families?

I see this time and again, and I see it in myself as well. When I 'm speaking in another town, I'm on my best behavior. Everyone gets a smile and a kind word from Tony Evans. But sometimes I've returned home and snapped at my wife and kids for no other reason than I'm just tired. I shrug it off and think, *Oh, they know me when I get like this. They'll let it slide.* Talk about taking people for granted!

Common courtesy is a lost art, even in

many Christian families. It doesn't take too much to offer a kind word or, every once in a while, clean up a mess around the house that you didn't make. The biggest love is often revealed in the smallest acts.

Men, remember when you were dating your wife and you couldn't wait to open the car door for her? Now she's lucky to get into the car before you drive off. Ladies, remember when you would go to great pains to fix your husband's favorite meal? Is he lucky now to get a TV dinner? Love doesn't forget the little things.

"Love takes no pleasure in other people's sins, but delights in the truth" (v. 6).

One of the most painful experiences of life is to watch a member of your own family stumble and fall while you're absolutely powerless to do anything about it. It's harder yet to watch the person suffer the consequences—to sit by helplessly and watch it happen. Yet we all know, if we think it through, that stumbling, falling, and getting back up again is a common part of spiritual (or any other kind of) growth.

I remember when Chrystal, my first child, was learning to walk. That was a very nervous time. Lois and I were caught in the tension of wanting to be close enough to catch her if she stumbled, yet far enough back that she had to take the risk of walking in order to get to us. There were some falls, and they probably hurt us worse than they hurt her, but we were usually close enough to cushion the blows.

The nature of life's knocks on children changes over time, but not our need as parents to give them room to grow, to comfort them when they fall, and to help them get back on their feet again.

"[Love] is always ready to excuse, to trust, to hope, and to endure whatever comes" (v. 7).

How many times do you bring up the past while correcting your children in the present, long after they have apologized and truly tried to live according to the rules you've set down? What does a child learn from that? Mom and Dad don't really forgive; they keep a running count of all misdeeds. What's the point, then, of doing what you're told if Mom and Dad are going to keep bringing up things from the past?

Likewise with your spouse. I can't even count the number of times during counseling sessions when I've heard a husband or wife refuse to acknowledge the present problem in their relationship and instead go back years in the past to dredge up an embarrassing moment that has long been atoned for. Then I hear the clincher. When I tell a couple we can proceed no further without some forgiveness being extended, one pipes up and says, "Well, I can forgive, but I certainly can't forget!"

Let me tell you a story about forgiving and letting go of things. One day, two monks were walking through the countryside. They were on their way to another village to help bring in the crops. As they walked, they spied an old woman sitting at the edge of a river. She was upset because there was no bridge, and she could not get across on her own.

The first monk kindly offered, "We'll carry you across if you'd like."

"Thank you," she said gratefully, accepting their help.

So the two men joined hands, lifted her between them, and carried her across the river. When they got to the other side, they set her down, and she went on her way.

After they had walked another mile or so, the second monk began to complain. "Look at my clothes," he said. "They're filthy from carrying that woman across the river. And my back still hurts from lifting her. I can feel it getting stiff."

The first monk just smiled and nodded his head.

A few more miles up the road, the second monk griped again, "My back is hurting me so badly, and it's all because we had to carry that silly woman across the river! I can't go any farther because of the pain."

The first monk looked down at his partner, now lying on the ground, moaning. "Have you wondered why I'm not complaining?" he asked. "Your back hurts because you're still carrying the woman. But I set her down five miles ago."

That's what many of us are like in dealing with our families. We're that second monk who can't let go. We hold the pain of the past over our loved ones' heads like a club, or we remind them every once in a while, when we want to get the upper hand, of the burden we still carry because of something they did years ago.

How grateful I am that God has told me that if I'm repentant and earnestly desire to turn my life around, He will "remember my sins no more." If He operated on the principles we often use with one another, we'd all be hell-bound on a fast track.

I know that true love and forgiveness work in families. While I've seen many families hold each other in bondage because of the sins of the past, I've also seen others hurdle incredible odds to forgive, forget, and restore a broken home. I've seen couples heal from the wreckage left by adulterous relationships; I've seen rebellious kids who have run off into a life of alcohol and drug abuse turn around; and I've watched with great joy as family and child worked together on the hard path of reconciliation.

The Most Important Thing

What 1 Corinthians 13 boils down to is unconditional love, love that is not based on your child's or spouse's performance, or on how you feel about your family on any given day.

As husbands and wives, we must never lose sight of that vow of unconditional love we gave each other in the wedding ceremony. The depth to which those vows are adhered will determine the spiritual strength of the marriage and of our kids.

· Children are vulnerable, sensitive. They're affected by our actions even when we think they may not notice. Dr. Ross Campbell, in his book *How to Really Love Your Child*, talks about those qualities in children and how we, as parents, can become more attuned to the signals they give us. He writes: "Almost every study I know indicates that any child is continually asking his parents, 'Do you love me?' A child asks this emotional question mostly in his behavior, seldom verbally. The answer to this question is absolutely the most important thing in any child's life.

"'Do you love me?' If we love a child unconditionally, he feels the answer to the question is yes. If we love conditionally, he is unsure, and again prone to anxiety. The answer we give a child to this all important question, 'Do you love me?' pretty well determines his basic attitude toward life. It's crucial."'[1]

Though Dr. M. Scott Peck admits that his definition of love is ultimately inadequate, I see a great deal of truth in it as written in his book *The Road Less Traveled:* "I define love thus: The will to extend one's self for the purpose of nurturing one's own or another's spiritual growth."[2]

In other words, love requires effort. The very word *extend* in Peck's definition makes that clear. Though good feelings, lifted emotions, and serenity may be known through love, Peck says they are not (as our culture tells us) the goal. The aim of love is to promote spiritual growth in ourselves and others, especially our families. Mom or Dad, extending yourself means more than simply teaching your children spiritual truth. *It also means modeling spiritual truth.*

Stay-at-home mothers, extending yourself may mean cutting down on church or recreational activities to be there when your kids get home from school. Fathers, it may mean turning down some career prestige if advancement will require you to spend a lot of time away from home.

The will to extend yourself is hard work. Our egos are strong, and we often would rather not make the hard choice of going out of our way for our families, especially if we feel we're giving a lot already. It's much more comfortable to sit in church and say "Amen" to a love sermon than to spend hours tutoring a child in spelling or math. It's a lot easier to stay busy in church activities all week than it is to go to your spouse or your children when you've done something to hurt them and admit you were wrong.

In the end, the truth about love is simple but biblical: Talk is cheap. Love is as love does.

CHAPTER FOUR

Family Honor, Family Respect

I'll never forget one of the big disappoint-ments of my childhood. I brought it on myself, and that only added to the pain.

My parents were adamant that my broth-ers and sisters and I be model students. Any disciplinary problems in our classes would be caused by *other people's kids*. Why was that so important to my folks? Because a teacher was someone to be highly respected and obeyed. Because the Evans family honor was at stake; what one child did reflected on us all. Because they were concerned about the kind of people into which we would grow. And because as Christians, we were to honor those God had placed in authority over us.

Mom and Dad also made it clear that if we misbehaved in school, there would be *consequences*. Believe me, my father cut his kids no slack when it came to breaking the rules. As much as I loved and respected him and knew he loved me, I also knew he would never fail to administer discipline when I had it coming. There are certain things I did not do simply because I didn't want to have to eyeball Dad afterward.

Well, as you've probably guessed by now, there came a day when I forgot all those things and really acted up in school. I misbehaved so badly that a call was placed to my father to tell him what his son Tony had done.

The penalty for such conduct was a spanking with Dad's razor strap plus the loss of some privilege. It just so happened that on that day, my school baseball team was playing an important game. I was the starting catcher. But after administering the spanking, Dad said those dreaded words: "No game for you today!"

You have to understand that I *love* baseball, and I was having a banner year. So to hear that I couldn't play that day nearly killed me. As if that weren't bad enough, however, I had to go tell the coach why I couldn't play, which embarrassed me almost to tears. And the worst part of all was that Dad finally said I could go outside and play again at six o'clock—right when the ball game would be ending.

That tale of youthful disappointment is only half the story, however. For while the incident caused me a lot of pain at the time, it also accomplished my father's purpose, which was far more important in the long run. It helped a great deal to teach me respect for my father, respect for my teachers, respect for authority generally, the importance of living within the "law," and the fact that there's a price to pay when you don't.

My father also "ruined" many a Saturday night in my youth by saying as I went out the front door, "Remember your last name is Evans." Obviously, he didn't need to remind me of my name. But he was reminding me that our name represented honesty, integrity in the community, morality, dignity, and honor. In short, it represented a commitment to Christian living, and Dad didn't want me to do anything to jeopardize our testimony. That reminder often changed my plans for the evening, because I respected my father and wanted to honor his name.

Not every child in my community was taught those lessons, and I see the results every year when I go back to inner-city Baltimore to visit my folks. Many of my boyhood friends are now dead, on drugs, or still just hanging out on the same street corner we hung out on as kids. But the respect and honor my parents instilled in me helped me to progress beyond the limitations of the neighborhood.

Teaching Respect

In the preceding chapter, I described love-in-action as foundational to guiding our families through this misguided world. In this chapter, I want to emphasize respect and honor as two more essential parts of the family's foundation.

In Scripture, honor and respect are first spoken of with regard to parents. Exodus 20:12 says, "Honor your father and your mother so that you may have a long life in the land your God has given you."

These days it's customary to blame your ills, your mistakes, and the way you behave in general on your parents. I like the story of the two brothers who went through a counseling session together. They had been brought up in a home where the father was a chronic alcoholic. One of the brothers had also become a chronic alcoholic, but the other drank nothing stronger than ice tea. When asked to explain their behavior, they said in unison, "Well, what else could you expect with a father like mine?"

We smile at the humorous side of that story, and we understand instinctively the serious side. Both boys told the truth: One followed their father's example, even though he probably didn't want to, and the other—the stronger—managed to stick to his resolve not to end up like their dad. The story also illustrates the truth that parents get blamed for far too much and receive praise for far too little.

The fact is, however, that we parents need to teach our children to respect and honor us and others, and we also have to earn that respect. Let me explain.

When my father disciplined me for acting up in school, as much as I disliked it, I grew in respect for him. He had given me plenty of warning that misbehavior in class would not be tolerated. He had always followed through on his warnings in the past. And by being consistent that day and spanking and grounding me, he was showing me once again that he was a man of his word; that his rules counted; that he was not a person to be trifled with. In short, he was a man to be respected at all times.

As the Bible says, "We have all had human fathers who disciplined us *and we respected them for it*" (Heb. 12:9, emphasis added). Proper discipline naturally creates respect, as God intended.

My father's first name is Arthur, but I would never call him that. To me he'll always be Dad. And when I take my family to visit him during our summer vacation, I'm once again under his authority while I'm in his house. My age makes no difference. That's the kind of respect I have for him.

Verbally and by his actions, Dad taught me to respect my teachers as well. Their job was so important and their position was so noble that I needed to do what they told me—and I would answer to him as well as to them if I didn't.

The alcoholic father I mentioned earlier probably didn't teach his sons to respect anyone, and he certainly didn't earn their respect for himself. That one of the boys turned out to lead a sober lifestyle was no credit to the dad but a miracle of grace instead.

Another failure of an adult to teach and earn respect haunts my memory. It wasn't a parent and child relationship, but it was in the church, which is almost as bad.

A boy about thirteen years old attended church regularly. He was in charge of a small equipment room where he taped the pastor's Sunday morning and Wednesday evening messages. This room was also where the ushers left the offering collection plates until the service was over.

One Sunday morning, a plate turned up missing. One of the ushers, who was also an elder, wasted no time in giving his opinion on who had taken the money—the young man in the equipment room. Who else could it be? The boy denied it, but no one was listening. After about fifteen minutes of frantic searching, however, the missing collection plate was found in the church office—where it had mistakenly been placed by the accusing elder.

The young man left the church that morning with his family. He returned for a time, but he eventually quit going entirely. Even though the accusation against him had been untrue, it broke his spirit to think he wasn't trusted.

Let's look at just what happened in that instance. Did the elder teach the boy respect? Did the elder earn any respect for himself (in the eyes of the boy or anyone else)? Did the elder honor the boy? The obvious answer to all these questions is no. Furthermore, *God* was dishonored, because one of His children was falsely accused and had his spirit crushed.

Proper discipline that instills respect takes time and effort on the part of us parents. The time and effort are needed to make sure we have all the facts straight before we act. We also have to *make* time and put forth the effort to discipline when there are a million other things we'd rather do, like put our feet up and relax at the end of a long, hard day.

Proper discipline requires one other thing, too: a long-term perspective. At the moment when discipline is needed, it's not pleasant for anyone. My father didn't enjoy spanking me, nor did I enjoy being on the receiving end. He didn't enjoy keeping me out of a ball game, either, knowing how much I love baseball. *But his thinking went way beyond what would make either of us happy at that moment.*

"No discipline seems pleasant at the time, but painful," we read in Hebrews 12:11. "Later on, however, it produces a harvest of righteousness and peace for those who have been trained by it." There's your long-term perspective.

God is looking down the road in disciplining us, Hebrews 12 says, keeping His eyes on the goal of making us more and more like Christ. And in the same way, we parents need to be looking at our kids not just in terms of what they're like now, but also in terms of the kind of men and women they'll be when they're grown and on their own.

I've taught my sons that when the Evans family sits down to dinner, they help their sisters to be comfortably seated at the table before they sit themselves—just as I do for their mother. Do the boys enjoy that? Are you kidding? Did I enjoy training them to do it, and do I like having to give them constant reminders now? Of course not. But my goal is not to keep everyone happy all the time. My goal is to raise sons who will treat women generally—and especially the women who will one day become their wives—with courtesy and respect at all times.

I'm thinking of my sons not just as the boys they are now, you see, but more importantly as the men they will be for a lifetime. I'm thinking, too, about the quality of relationships they'll enjoy all those years. And in that light, I'm willing to pay the price to train them properly, just as my parents paid the price to discipline me.

The end result is that I—not the guys who refer to their wives as "my old lady"—am the one who establishes how my boys think women should be treated. I'm also showing my daughters they should not be satisfied with any man who doesn't respect them enough to put their comfort above his own.

I recently received a wonderful compliment. I was visiting one of my sons' teachers at school, and she told me that in her fifteen years of teaching, she has never had as gentlemanly a student as my son. He even refuses to enter the classroom until he has held the door open for her, she said. Boy, was I proud!

Giving Respect

But parents, I am also a realist. There are many times we make it hard for our children to honor and respect us: for example, when we're inconsistent with our discipline, when we favor one child over another, and when our children hear us gossiping about others. Invoking the biblical mandate isn't enough. Although the command is all, inclusive and, by implication, calls on children to honor their parents unconditionally, I believe that this honor must be mutual.

One way we honor and respect our children is by remaining teachable, which requires humility. (If you think children have nothing to teach you, you probably don't have any children yet.)

Consider the arena of organized sports. Have you ever watched an organized baseball game featuring a bunch of seven- and eight-year-olds? The kids are feeling all puffed up in their uniforms (which are usually a couple of sizes too large), striking out, dropping the ball, and throwing the ball over everyone's head. Even a routine grounder to the second baseman is a potential home run. The kids are having a great time. To them it's just a game.

But to the parents? Every game is like the seventh game of the World Series! They bark directions to the coaches, overrule them, yell at the umpires, and do a slow burn if their child's team loses a game. The kids may have had a great time with their buddies, but their parents are getting ulcers.

Who's teaching whom in that situation?

Another way we honor and respect our children is by making certain we practice what we preach. Though it's a rather extreme example, I think of the television commercial in which an angry father confronts his son with some marijuana he's found in the boy's room. The father badgers the child, saying, "Who gave this to you? Who taught you how to use this stuff?"

The son looks up and shouts, "It was you and Mom! I saw you both use it!"

A young child will imitate his parents no matter what their behavior may be. The most humorous (painfully so) examples I've seen of this are in the "Dennis the Menace" cartoons in the newspaper. In one instance, Dennis's mother is talking to another woman. Dennis looks inquisitively at the guest and then remarks, "I don't see anything coming out of her mouth, Mom. You said she talked a blue streak."

In another strip, Dennis and his family are greeting the pastor after church, and Dennis says, "I brought these three rocks to church today because my dad said you could put a stone to sleep!"

If we want to give our children honor and respect, then, we'll be careful about the example we set and the consistency we show between our words and our actions.

Being There

My ministry is primarily to urban communities throughout the United States, and one of the issues that has to be addressed there is poverty. It comes in two forms: economic poverty and a poverty of hope. I was fortunate when I was growing up. I had a father who was a positive role model, someone I could look up to. Many young black men and women today are not as fortunate. In the black community in 1991, more than 50 percent of the children were growing up without a father in the home. An article in the *U.S. News and World Report* of September 24, 1990, said that in the overwhelmingly black Harlem district of New York City, the number rises to 80 percent.

To children in such communities, what does "Honor thy father" mean? One of my biggest burdens is to develop strong, black, male, Christian leadership—men who will serve as mentors and role models to young black men and women who have never known what it's like to have a father in the home.

The problem of missing fathers isn't unique to the black community, however. More than 50 percent of the households nationwide are now single-parent homes. We have come to a day in our culture that used to seem unthinkable: There are more families broken apart than together, and the odds are better than even that if you get married, you won't stay married.

Even in families that do stay together, many of the children grow up with strangers, because Mom and Dad are both consumed with making a living. How do we instill any values, including respect and honor, when we're just not available to our children?

Let me tell you the story of a young man. I pray your kids will never experience what he has. I'd like to assume they never will, but the hard, unavoidable statistics make that a dangerous assumption. Even if your children are spared such pain, however, you probably know someone with a similar story. Your child may marry such a person. You may be that someone yourself.

Fred loved his father. Dad was always there for him. He coached his Little League teams; they went for rides together; they talked a lot. Fred's dad also worked a lot of extra hours to provide the family with what they needed, even if they had to scrimp at times.

Fred went through college. He and his dad stayed in touch. Things seemed to be going fine. Then one day, right out of the blue, Dad was gone. Mom said the two of them were getting a divorce. It turned out that some of the idyllic things Fred thought about his dad were wrong. Even though at times Fred had sensed something was wrong, he had always chosen to deny what he saw and felt.

For the next eleven years, Fred hated his father. He wanted nothing to do with him. He went to church a lot, however, and heard "Honor thy father" a lot.

"Not my father," he said. "How could I ever respect him after what he's done?"

It was a very slow road on the way to forgiveness. There was no real love anymore. As he looked back, Fred felt he never really knew any more about his father than name, rank, and serial number.

Fred was living in another state, far away from his family. He was immersed in his own life, interested only in "getting on with it." His was a restless spirit that couldn't seem to find one place and make it home. Fred had good jobs, but he just kept drifting.

Then Fred started to notice another pattern in his behavior. Everywhere he went, he seemed to locate someone about his father's age in whom he could confide. He would always feel secure around these men; they were his life's anchor. After a time, however, it dawned on him that the man he really needed to talk with was two thousand miles away.

Fred went home with some vacation time he had. While he was there, he visited his father. And they began to talk—really talk. Fred felt as if he was meeting his father for the first time. And there were tears also, because Fred was able to see that for all his frailties, his father was a loving man who, like all of us, simply wanted to be understood and loved. The bitterness of resentment and unforgiveness fell away from Fred one afternoon. He could say the word *father* again without hurting.

About seven months later, Fred had to travel to another state on a business trip that would last a week. One of those days was a special day to Fred, but because he was on the road, he decided to keep quiet about it. That afternoon, however, while he was deep into a project, the phone rang. The operator said she had a call for him. When Fred said hello, these were the words he heard:

"Happy birthday, Son."

Those words marked the beginning of a real relationship, at long last, between Fred and his father. So in that sense the story has a happy ending. But the reconciliation came only after years of pain and lost opportunity. Fred's dad would never have the kind of influence on his son that all dads yearn for.

How do we teach our children to treat people with honor and respect? How do we guide them through a society that treats people like commodities? It begins with making an intentional effort to teach them. It continues with a willingness to train (discipline) them, correcting them with an eye to the men and women they will become. And most important of all, it hinges on our example.

Children won't always do what they're told, but they'll do what they see. If they see you treat your spouse disrespectfully; if they hear you gossip about friends or people in the church; if they see you treating your parents like a burden, then don't be surprised if they grow up to do the same. This matter of our parental example is so crucial that it's the subject of the entire next chapter.

I have to close *this* chapter, however, with a story that makes me think the principles I'm presenting can truly help your family. Chrystal, my older daughter, recently called me from college. "Dad," she said, "I was at a women's retreat over the weekend, and they asked us, 'If you died in the next twenty-four hours, what would you regret never having done?'"

She went on to say that the first thought that had come to her mind was to call her mom and dad and tell us how much she loved us and how thankful she was for the time, energy, love, and discipline we had given her. She added that even though she hasn't always been the perfect daughter, she realizes her stability, character, and Christian standards and commitment are a reflection of the investment we've made in her life. She closed by saying, "I didn't want this to be the last night of my life and not have taken the opportunity to say how grateful I am for Mom's and your love."

I can't tell you what a great sense of satisfaction her words gave me, and I'm sure you'd be thrilled to hear the same kind of sentiments from your children. I'm so glad a legacy of hope has been transferred to our child, and I believe you can do the same for yours.

CHAPTER FIVE

Someone's Watching You

When I see something that's worth getting excited about, I get excited! I show it! No one who knows me well will ever describe me as "laid back." As my wife often remarks, I'm just like my father in that regard. And Anthony, Jr., is just like his grandfather and father.

When she's reacting to something negative or doesn't like what she's hearing, Lois has a habit of making a sort of hissing sound by breathing in through her teeth. She picked that up from her mom. And now our daughter Chrystal has developed the same habit.

No doubt you've also found yourself at different times performing some little quirk or mannerism, or saying something in a particular way, only to stop suddenly and exclaim, "Oh my word, that's just the way

Mom (or Dad) did that!" It can be a little unnerving, especially if the mannerism or saying really annoyed you when your parent did it.

Unfortunately, not all the habits children pick up from their parents are so benign. You may recall the true-to-life TV commercial of a few years ago in which a young boy is out walking with his father. As they go along, the boy tries to do everything just like Dad.

When Dad picks up a stone and gives it a toss, the boy does the same. When Dad purposely scuffles up dirt with his feet, the son follows suit. It's a charming scene. But then the father sits down, leans against a tree, lights up a cigarette, and drops the pack to the ground beside him. And sure enough, the boy sits down, picks up the pack, and tries to take out a cigarette.

The commercial closes with the announcer's saying, "Your son wants to be just like you."

I would guess that most people reading this book don't smoke. But do we model materialism for our kids? How about hypocrisy, selfishness, the use of anger to get our way, a cutting tongue? Our children want to be just like us.

Most authorities in the field of child psychology and behavior will tell you that a child's personality, self-esteem, and behavior patterns are pretty well formed by the age of four or five. I used to think that was ridiculous, but I don't anymore. I think back to when our four children were infants. I remember how their eyes would dart between their mother and me when we were in a room with them. When they were in a room full of adults, their eyes would do that same quick dance.

It finally dawned on me one day—our children are not casual observers. They take in the whole scene; they watch everybody, but especially their parents; they're sponges, soaking it all in. By the time they're four or five, they've surveyed the situation pretty well. They know whether to feel positive or negative about themselves (based on what we've said and how we've treated them); how to treat people (based on how they've seen us treat others); and they know whether or not dishonest behavior will get them what they want (based on how we've responded to it).

Children are listening when we think they're not listening, and they're watching when we think they're not watching. I recently heard of a sad example that brings this point home. One summer at a church youth camp, an interesting story began circulating. A camper had noticed that someone's dad was paying more attention than usual to the mom of one of the other campers.

No doubt the father in question had taken pains to keep hidden his illicit affections. He probably thought he was doing a good job of disguising his actions. But he wasn't fooling anyone, least of all the kids.

Regardless of what we try to teach by precept or by story, our greatest influence as parents will come through the example we set. That's why, as one wise person said, "The first great gift we can bestow on others is a good example." Conversely, as an old Persian proverb says, "If the teacher be corrupt, the world will be corrupt." No matter how good the content of our verbal lessons, our children will learn primarily from the way we live.

Beginning at Birth

From a physical standpoint, birth is a traumatic experience. The mother's body is repeatedly taut, then convulsed, and the child is pushed through a narrow birth canal and out into the world. Immediately, its tie with the mother's life-support system is cut, and it is exposed and vulnerable.

I'm convinced that both parents need to be in that delivery room, because then, right from the beginning, the child will have two focal points—two sets of arms holding it, two sets of hands touching it, two voices speaking to it lovingly. From the moment of birth, both parents are the center of its universe. The child will watch them like a hawk and take its cues from them. Other people will be important, but only insofar as they relate to the parents. Even though a child may be cooing or giggling or laughing, it's busy filing away information that says, in essence, "If that's how Mom and Dad do it, that must be the way I should do it."

As our children grow, we adults can get pretty cagey at times. For example, when young children are around and we want to make sure they don't know what we're talking about, we spell the word, or words, we don't want them to understand: "Did you hear what Mrs. Smith said in church last Sunday about the visitation committee? I don't believe I've heard anything so s-t-u-p-i-d in my whole life."

When we do that, we may think we're putting something over on our kids, but we're really not. What they understand clearly is that we're trying to hide something from them.

I go back to the point I made in the preceding chapter: Our kids need to see consistency in our lives. Dad, if you're a tyrant at home but you put on the mask of a saint at church, your young children won't get upset at you. Because you're their role model, they'll probably think that's perfectly acceptable behavior. When you punish them for saying one thing and doing another, however, they won't understand. After all, they saw you behave that way, and no one punished you!

Let's consider the dinner table—that all-important place where a lot of the family business is conducted. What is our conversation like there? Is it spent building up one another or others, or is it a gossip session in which we concentrate on the negatives? If we spend most of our time criticizing others, should we really be surprised when our children talk back to us?

It bears repeating again: Our kids learn from us mostly by our actions. If our words are different from our actions, our children will give the most weight to what we do.

Kids also learn from how they're treated. If our love, displays of affection, and caring are conditional, our children will grow up thinking they are worthy only to the extent that they please us and do what we want.

I don't know how many times I've cringed inwardly when I've heard parents casually remark to their children, "Mommy and Daddy won't love you if you do that." Earlier I explained that the central question of a child's life—a question he or she is asking all the time, in all words and actions—is

"Do you love me?" A comment such as the one above, no matter how innocently it's made, tells a child that the parents' love is conditional. Being their child simply isn't enough to make the child worthy of love.

A child who grows up with conditional love will practice conditional love. Worse yet, such a child is very likely to believe in a God who also practices conditional love, especially when He is given the parental title of *Father*.

False Cues from the World—and the Church

Kids need good role models—heroes. As their parents, we should be their first and foremost models. But we should also be aware that our misguided world—and even misguided Christians—are eagerly offering them alternatives.

Our culture tells our children that in order to be important, to be admired and respected, you have to be famous, powerful, and beautiful. You have to make a lot of money, and you have to make it quickly, like an entertainer or a professional athlete.

I'm not throwing a blanket condemnation over athletes and entertainers; many of them provide excellent role models. But those who do are worthy of kids' respect because of how they conduct their lives, not because of how they make their money or how much of it they make.

Our children are listening to what society tells them is important. As parents, we need to let them know that the size of a person's celebrity or bank account isn't nearly as significant as the depth of a person's character. We must teach them more about the everyday heroes—folks in the neighborhood who go to work each day, who perform society's not-so-glamorous tasks, who give of themselves for the benefit of others. As Christian singer and songwriter Bill Gaither says, "They have names few would recognize, but they'll be no surprise to the saints in glory."

Gaither wrote about one of these heroes: "Our company comptroller, Dan Lacey, displays the expected qualities of a hard-nosed businessman. But recently I saw him in a new light as I passed our church kindergarten one Sunday. There was Dan, surrounded by a swarm of eager children.

"'Helping out?' I asked.

"'No,' he corrected. 'I'm teaching.'

"'Oh? For how long?' I asked. His answer surprised and delighted me.

"'A couple of years now,' he said. His reply was warm and enthusiastic. He obviously loved these kids, and they loved him.

"The secular media—and many in the church—would pass by Dan's devotion without notice. But it's time to start recognizing the hidden heroes of the kingdom. Not to stroke their egos, but to draw attention to their service in such a way as to encourage others to emulate them." [1]

I cite this example because it's so unusual. And the Christian culture falls short here as well. It disturbs me to see us make "super Christians" out of athletes and media celebrities. What's even more disturbing is how quickly we do it. Such people often seem to be yanked up from their knees as soon as they've prayed to accept Christ. If a highly visible person becomes a Christian, conversion is quickly followed by a hastily put together biography, a series of appearances on Christian programs, and cover stories in Christian magazines. We want to hold this person up to the light and show the world that one of their own has "defected" to the other side. We then offer this star as an example for our children to follow.

By doing this, we do a disservice to both our children and the celebrity. For the new Christian, there is a tremendous amount of pressure to keep up a facade, to appear never to falter or seem to be anything but totally in control.

We have also ignored what I call the doctrine of preparation. Moses is one example. His life up until the time he was eighty was spent in preparation for God's calling him to lead the children of Israel out of slavery.

The apostle Paul, after his dramatic conversion on the Damascus Road, spent more than three years in preparation for his public ministry—not exactly an overnight sensation.

Our Savior's entire public ministry was only three years long. His life prior to that was spent working as a carpenter and maturing into the Man who would follow the Father's will all the way to the cross.

Frankly, I think our current celebrity fixation is indulged in more to boost our own egos than for any other reason. Often it pains me to look at what Christian books and magazines are offering—each year it seems they play the game of who can come up with the biggest name for the publishing season.

How are we to tell our children not to live by the world's standards when they see us creating these "super Christians" and putting them on pedestals? What we're telling them is that if you're a Christian, God loves you; but if you're a top athlete or an entertainer and a Christian, God loves you *a lot*.

Children who use this false barometer of success as a guide to life will probably end up frustrated when their experiences don't mirror the lives of the heroes the church sets before them. The saddest result of all this spiritual celebrity stuff, however, may be that kids will blame God for their disappointments.

Let me suggest, then, that we give our children more everyday heroes to emulate. I think of my wife's single sister, Elizabeth, who lives a morally exemplary life. She's a great example of Christian womanhood and offers my daughters an appealing alternative to the Madonna mania of modern culture. I also recall a missionary family who were guests in our home and whose stories challenged my whole family to consider what true commitment means. Other heroes include local church leaders, widows who have raised their families successfully, and teachers who have invested so much in us and our kids.

Your Actions, Your Lifestyle

As we think about the kind of role models we're giving our children, we need to be aware of some common, subtle practices within the family that could have dangerous repercussions if they're not dealt with now. Here are some examples:

1. Do you encourage discussion in your family—about all matters? If your ten-year-old daughter comes up to you and asks about sex, do you say, "You're not old enough to know about that yet. When it's the right time, we'll tell you"? That child will go out and have her inquisitiveness satisfied. It may not be you, however, who provides the information.

2. *If your children question your behavior and you know you've done wrong, do you get defensive or remark, "When you're an adult, you'll understand better"?* That's a dodge, and your kids know it. Their respect for you will grow geometrically if you're man or woman enough to admit you've made a mistake.

3. *Do you allow your children to see you when you're hurt, when you're crying, or do you try to hide it from them?* Sadly, I've met some Christian parents who feel it's a sign of weakness to show any emotion or hurt, the justification being that their children will see them as unstable. What sort of bill of goods have we sold ourselves?

One of the most beautiful verses in Scripture is also the shortest. Jesus was told His friend Lazarus had died. And what does the verse say? It simply records our Lord's natural, human (and divine) reaction: "Jesus wept" (John 11:35). I'm sure that anyone who knew Him did not begin to think, *Hey, why is Jesus wimping out on us like this? He needs to be strong for us!*

Fathers, me included, need to hear this: "Big boys do cry." Strong Christian men don't ever need to be ashamed of their tears. We are human, and our children will discover this sooner or later, whether we want them to or not. I think of the sad, sad story I've heard from many Christian brothers and sisters as they buried their fathers. They've told me through their own tears, "Tony, I'm nearly middle-aged myself, and I never, ever saw that man cry." They were saying it with profound remorse, not listing it as a character strength.

How?

What I have told you might seem intimidating. Do this, don't do that, watch your step here, look out for this, look out for that. You might be wondering now, *How can I set a good example without becoming paranoid about the effect of the mistakes I'll inevitably make?*

In a way, being a parent is intimidating; we've been placed in charge of developing and nurturing other lives. How our children grow will in many ways be due to our influence. A lot of parents walk into it lightly. All of us who are parents, however, soon learn the gravity of the responsibility we've taken on. This chapter is not a call to be perfect, however, but a call to remain aware.

Now the question: How do we do all that God has asked of us as parents without falling into the trap of perfectionism or false pride? The answer, I believe, is contained in the acronym HOW.

First, we need *honesty*. That covers a lot of territory. God does not expect us to show up every morning ready for another day of perfect parenting. But He does expect us to be honest about our shortcomings and limitations. Only then will our example have credibility with our kids. And only when we're honest about our own limitations will we be able to accept those of our children and offer them unconditional love.

One of the best examples of parenting I've seen in this area involves a man who is now in his early forties. He said, "I felt bad for a lot of my friends when I was growing up. Their parents were pretty tough on them when it came to grades in school. Their parents were crushed when they came home with B's instead of A's. They got grounded whenever their grades weren't at the top. What was funny was that the more the parents grounded the kids, the more they rebelled. Some of them even got further behind in school.

"I'll never forget one day when I was in my last year of elementary school. I came home from school with a report card that had three C's on it. I had no idea what I would face. My father looked at the card, however, and said, 'Three C's. Now let me see. Where on this card does it tell me what a C means?

Oh, here it is. C means "average." To me, average means "just fine." Average means "okay." I don't see anything wrong with having an average, okay son.'

"Dad would also say, 'Did you try your best on this subject?' Because I knew how he felt toward me, I always answered him honestly. If I said yes, he would say, 'If you did your best, you can be proud of yourself. '

"It's funny—when he told me that being an average ten-year-old was okay with him, I felt as loved as I've ever felt in my entire life. I wanted to do my best for him because all he honestly wanted me to be was a skinny little ten-year-old, not a miniature adult."

The second part of HOW is *openness*—something a parent needs for survival. In many cases, we don't start getting open until we're pushed or someone forces it out of us at the dinner table at exactly the wrong time.

Openness is a great release valve on that steam cooker I call perfectionism. It works like this: We don't push ourselves too hard in pursuit of impossible standards of performance. When we've had enough, we say we've had enough; we don't say everything's fine when it isn't; we don't tell our children something's okay when it's not; when there's a strain between us and our spouse or children, we talk it out before we snap and use anger as a weapon.

Each of these actions releases pressure and keeps things from building to the explosion point. Each of them also provides an example to our children of healthy parenting and healthy living in general.

Sadly, we often don't take advantage of the one place where we're the most free to be open, either—in prayer before God. I've had times when my whole body was filled to the top of my skull with anger. I was a walking time bomb; I knew I needed to pray. What did I do? I got on my knees, stuffed my anger, and began a pious monologue to my Creator. I could have been praying in the pulpit on Sunday morning.

The hymn "What a Friend We Have in Jesus" says, "What a privilege to carry everything to God in prayer." That line echoes 1 Peter 5:7: "Cast all your anxiety on him because he cares for you." But as the hymn goes on to say, we instead needlessly bear great pain because we don't take God up on that offer.

Prayer is a time for openness. It can ease the sufferings and frustrations of parenthood more than we can possibly imagine. Yet we often shut ourselves off from the peace God can provide because we refuse to acknowledge to Him how we're feeling.

The final letter in the acronym HOW refers to *willingness*. As parents, we are regularly called upon to make the hard decisions concerning discipline, advice we should give, and flaws in our character we want to change. God knows parenting isn't easy, and He knows we struggle to live consistent lives and provide godly models for our kids. But I've found that if I am genuinely willing for God to make over a certain area of my life, it will happen. He will acknowledge my willingness and give me the strength to work toward change. His presence has been strongest when what I needed to change in me seemed most hopeless.

Honesty, openness, and willingness are crucial to providing the kind of parental example our children will respect and recognize as genuine. Those qualities are also the tools that will comfort us and guide us through our imperfections rather than burden us with them. When we're honest, open, and willing, our children will see that although we may stumble and sometimes fall, we are seeking God and doing our best.

And just when you begin to think children don't understand any of this, they do.

CHAPTER SIX

Giving Our Children a Living Faith

Not long ago (it seems like yesterday), Lois and I went through something that eventually comes to all parents. For the first time, we sent our oldest child out into the world on her own. On an autumn day, we took Chrystal and her most essential worldly possessions off to college. It was an exciting day in many ways, but it also gave me pause for a great deal of thought.

Is she ready for this? I asked myself. *Is she prepared to be on her own? Can she face both temptations and opportunities and make wise decisions? Most importantly, is the faith her mother and I have instilled in her a genuine, personal faith that will stand her in good stead day in and day out, or has she really just gone through the motions because she thought that's what Lois and I wanted?*

The answers to all those questions, I knew, would come soon enough. Fortunately, because of what I had seen in her life, I was confident Chrystal's faith and maturity were ready for full adulthood (though I asked myself the questions anyway out of fatherly concern). But as we're raising our kids, we have to keep in mind that the day will come when they go out on their own, no longer under our direct supervision. Will they be prepared?

It should be evident to Christian parents that when our kids reach that point of making their own way in the world, the most important thing they'll need to take with them is a living, personal faith in Jesus Christ. They'll need to know how to pray, for example, for their own concerns and for others'. Even more crucial, they'll need to have a desire to pray when there's no one around to make them do it.

God Has No Grandchildren

Helping our children develop such a faith isn't easy, and it's certainly not automatic just because the family goes to church together on Sundays. We can't simply teach them faith the way we can teach math.

Christian psychologist Dr. Donald Sloat explains the difficulty this way: "Each person enters the world with no prior knowledge or experiences, which means each generation is starting out from scratch in attempting to deal with life. Fortunately, technical knowledge accumulates from one generation to the next. For example, the technology regarding the refining of gasoline and the engineering features of internal combustion engines has been developed and recorded by previous generations. Because new generations can study these principles, they do not have to reinvent everything from the wheel to computers, which saves them years of time.

"Christian values and knowledge about living accumulate as well. But unlike technical knowledge, they cannot be passed simply from one generation to the next because they have to become personally meaningful in an individual's life and experience. This requires years of living and learning from successes as well as mistakes. Since we all tend to learn the hard way from our own experiences rather than from our parents' experiences, we often repeat the mistakes of prior generations; hence the expression 'History repeats itself.'"[1]

I could tell you about many good, sincere Christian parents whose kids seem to have rejected the faith. They know all too well, from painful experience, that our kids don't automatically make our faith in Christ their own. Being believers in no way guarantees our children will choose the same course. God truly has no grandchildren.

So what can we do to steer our children in the right direction—to increase the likelihood that when they're making their own decisions, they'll make wise ones based on mature faith? From my study and experience, I believe there are five key things we can do.

Pray

The natural human tendency, even among Christians, is to think of prayer as a last resort. When we have a need or a problem, we consider what we can do and then work at it in our own power. Only when the situation seems hopeless do we decide, "We need to pray about this."

If we were thinking straight, however, prayer would be our *first* response to a need. So let me remind us all that prayer is an appeal to the sovereign God of the universe. There is no higher or more powerful source of help. As Alfred, Lord Tennyson said many years ago, "More things are wrought by prayer than this world dreams of." Or as an anonymous writer has said, "Satan trembles when he sees/The weakest saint upon his knees."

The best and most effective thing we can ever do for our children and families is to pray for them every day. Therefore, let me recommend a prayer habit that you can begin tonight. After your children have gone to sleep, go to their beds in order, and on your knees beside them, pray for your kids. Watch them sleep as you're praying. Rare will be the evening you do this that the tears don't come. Pray this way every night.

What specifically should you pray about? Let's look at Luke 2:52, which describes the boyhood of Jesus, for some ideas: "And Jesus kept increasing in wisdom and stature, and in favor with God and men."

Four areas of development are mentioned there, and they are all areas in which we'd like to see our children grow. The first is wisdom—not just factual knowledge, important as that is, but also biblical wisdom (the ability to apply knowledge to the practical issues of life). "The fear of the Lord is the beginning of wisdom; a good understanding have all those who do His commandments" (Ps. 111:10).

Pray, then, for your children's ability to do their best in school and grow intellectually. But even more importantly, pray that they'll grow in their reverence for the Lord and in their ability to know right (God's will) from wrong and to choose to do what's right.

"Increasing in … stature" refers to physical growth. Pray here for your kids' safety and good health so they can develop to the full extent of their God-given abilities.

"In favor with God" is a clear reference to spiritual growth. Pray that your children will always have tender hearts toward the Lord, that knowing Him, walking with Him, and serving Him will be their greatest desires. Pray also that true Christlikeness will be developed in them as time goes by.

Finally, "in favor with … men" refers to social growth. Pray that your kids will learn how to get along with others, how to be true friends, but without compromising their values. Pray that God will bring them good friends who will be a positive influence. And pray that even now, God would be preparing the boys and girls who will grow up to one day be godly mates for your children.

Seize the Day

The story is told of a young demon who came to Satan one day. He wanted to impress the devil with his ability to carry out the master's will. "I have a strategy that will keep Christians from following God," he said. "I'll convince them there is no God."

Satan just smiled and wished the young demon success.

A few days later, the demon returned dejected, his face downcast. "I couldn't get many Christians to believe there's no God," he admitted. But then he brightened and added, "However, I've got a better idea. I'll convince them there's no heaven!"

Again Satan smiled and sent the eager demon on his way.

After another few days, the demon returned once more with defeat written all over him. "I don't understand it," he told the Evil One. "What am I doing wrong? What's the secret of subverting Christians?"

Satan, who had been waiting for that moment, put his arm around the young intern's shoulders and explained, "Son, you can't succeed by trying to get them to deny the foundations of their faith. That's much too obvious an approach, and they'll reject it every time. I've been most successful over these many years by convincing them *there's no need to hurry* in living out their faith. I simply keep getting them to wait."

That's exactly what Satan has done in many of our families. He's made us into master procrastinators. We wait too long to strengthen and nurture our marriages, and our divorce rate is now approaching that of the secular world. We ignore the discipline and spiritual training of our kids until it's too late and we're leaving them on their own at that faraway college. We always think there's more time—there will be time enough tomorrow, when we're not so tired or we've finished that important work project or the holidays are over. And we play right into the devil's hands.

In a recent hit movie called *Dead Poet's Society,* Robin Williams plays a prep school English teacher who, early in the school year, takes his students into the hall of their old and prestigious school and shows them the framed pictures of graduating classes from decades ago. "Move up close to the pictures," he tells them. "Those boys were young and intelligent and full of dreams like you. They were just like you.

"They're all dead now," he continues. "They've turned into dust. But lean close; they're calling out to you. Listen. They're telling you, 'Carpe diem,' 'Seize the day.' Can you hear them? 'Carpe diem, carpe diem.'"

The message was clear, and it applies even more to us as spouses and parents. Life is passing fast, so make every day count. Live it to the fullest. Don't let an opportunity pass to do good, to build your relationships, to advance God's kingdom here on earth. Make the most of every day.

I'm not suggesting we need to panic about finding time to do everything we should, because the good news is that we have all the time we need. Think of the most productive person you know, the one who gets all kinds of work done and also has a healthy family life. Do you realize that you have just as much time available to you as that person? You do—we all do. We all get the same twenty-four hours each day, seven days a week.

Seizing the day, then, doesn't have to do with time so much as it has to do with *priorities*. The fact is that we always make time for the things that are most important to us, whether or not we understand that's what we're doing.

One day a few years ago, Lois told me I wasn't spending enough time with our kids. I had kind of been feeling that way myself, but I had tried to ignore the uncomfortable idea. So I said a little defensively, "I just wish I had more time, more hours in the day. I've got so much to do!" I quickly learned that was the wrong answer.

"You fly 30,000 miles a year preaching to people around the country," she said. "If you cut back on the number of trips you make, you'd have more time."

End of lesson? No, she was only starting. "You also work late at the church four nights a week. If you would delegate more and stop acting as if God had two saviors of the world, you'd have more time. Even when you are home, the phone rings off the hook, and you always pick it up. If you'd take the phone off the hook when you're with your family, you'd have more time for us."

Lois has a way of getting right to the heart of a matter, and she was on target again this time. My problem with shortchanging my family had little to do with time and almost everything to do with my priorities. Without realizing it, I had put my idea of what it meant to be a great pastor and preacher—my ego mixed in with God's calling—above my calling to be a great dad. That was a bad, albeit unconscious, decision.

My older son brought the same point home to me one day. I noticed he had a dejected look, so I asked him what was wrong. All he did was grunt. After I practically pulled teeth to get an answer, he finally told me, "Every time I want to talk to you, you're so busy counseling other people."

That was like a dagger in my heart. The very thing I had preached against I was doing to my son, and I was justifying it in the name of *ministry*.

I remembered how the great prophet Samuel had lost his children because he spent so much time on the road (see 1 Sam. 7:16; 8:1-5). I also recalled how Eli, the high priest, had forfeited his ministry and his very life because he had ignored his responsibility to discipline and train his sons (see 1 Sam. 2:12-17, 22-25; 3:10-18).

Clearly, I needed to reorder my priorities. I didn't want the world to become my kids' new father, nor did I want Lois to have to try being both mother *and* father to them. So with my blessing, Lois took out my appointment book and, like a mobster with a submachine gun, began to mow down engagement after engagement and meeting after meeting. I also committed to always being home for dinner on certain days of the week, and I told my secretary to let my kids through whenever they needed me. I'm happy to say that I've stayed with my new priorities, and I now have more time for those who count most—my wife and children.

What about your priorities and your schedule? Do you find yourself saying "Tomorrow" a lot? "Honey, tomorrow I'll spend time with you." "Kids, tomorrow I'll take some time to play with you." "Family, both Mom and Dad need to be away from home right now because we need the extra money. It won't be for long, kids. Just till we can get on our feet financially."

Too often, when those tomorrows come, the husband has left the home and the kids don't feel like hanging around the house much anymore. Forget about tomorrow. I like the old saying that goes, "Send me my flowers while I'm still alive."

I think of a former leader in our church—Pastor Carl. Death was at work in his body, but we didn't know it. We worked, fellowshipped, and played together. Today, as I look back, I wish I had complimented him more on his spirit and job performance. I wish I had spent more time with him, letting him know just how much his leadership meant to the church.

I can wish all I want, but I can't turn back the clock. At the age of thirty-four, Pastor Carl died of cancer.

Death was at work inside my dear brother, and I didn't know it. He looked fine from the outside. Many of our Christian families also look fine from the outside. Mom and Dad and two well-scrubbed kids are always in church on Sunday morning, always ready to volunteer for whatever needs to be done. Outside the church, however, Mom and Dad may not be speaking to each other, and the kids may not listen to a word their parents say. But when it's time to hit the front door of the church, the smiles are on and everything's fine.

A young man I know once threw a large monkey wrench into a Sunday morning service. He was a member of the high-school youth group and had been asked to talk about family relationships.

Now, teenagers aren't usually savvy enough to be "diplomatic." So this young man started talking. He went on for a few minutes before he dropped the bomb: "Everything looks fine in our family right now, but you should have seen the fight we had on the way over here this morning. It's like that most of the time."

His parents wanted to crawl under their seats; a lot of other parents looked at each other uneasily.

For a few more years, the young man's family kept up appearances, going to all the church functions, including the big event of the year, the candlelight service on Christmas Eve. In his last year of high school, his mom and dad and sister and brother were all at the service. But as time went on, his sister got married, his parents got divorced, and his brother simply drifted away. On Christmas Eve of his senior year in college, he was at the candlelight service again. He heard the prayers, listened to the bells, and held his candle high as he sang "Silent Night."

He was by himself.

Families don't fall apart all at once; it can take years. Communication doesn't stop in an instant; it disappears by bits until it's gone. Discipline doesn't break down overnight; it starts with one small inconsistency that leads to another and then another.

For the most part, this decay is caused by procrastination. We bask in the glow of a new marriage and think, *I've got a lot of time to work on this.* We bring a new son or daughter home from the hospital and say to ourselves, *Just think of all the years we're going to have with each other!*

Speaking as one spouse to another and one parent to another, let me make two simple observations: One year in a marriage will go by before you've had time to blink; and one evening at the dinner table, it will suddenly dawn on you that the young lady or gentleman sitting across from you is about to graduate from high school.

We have only one block of time in which to nurture our families, in which to build communication, in which to instill biblical principles and consistent discipline.

Today. It's all our Lord promised us.

Today. Seize it.

Worship

As a pastor, I have to say that far too many of us Christians are taking it easy spiritually. We're much too casual about our own faith and the biblical training of our kids. We believe we can sit back and let faith serve as our protective shield; we're slack in our prayer, our fellowship, and our study of

Scripture. We relax on the disciplines our faith calls us to and believe, naively, that we have it made. We ignore, or stuff into the background, our family problems and say, "The Lord will take care of His own." I know this attitude; I've been guilty of it myself.

If we neglect the spiritual condition of our families, however, we can be sure the devil and this world won't do the same. That fact alone, if nothing else, should give us the incentive we need to provide for our families' spiritual welfare. One key way we do that is family worship that goes beyond attending church together. Church services are an important starting point, but Sunday school, AWANA, Pioneer Clubs, and other programs should supplement, not substitute for, family worship.

What I'm advocating—what Lois and I have done with our children from the beginning—is what used to be called family devotions or the family altar. We've found the traditional times of right after breakfast or dinner work well, since we're all together at that point and we can make a little time for it before we go on to other plans for the day. Many families now schedule a family night each week, where the whole evening is devoted to family fun as well as worship.

For such a practice to work, several things need to be kept in mind. First, what you do has to be geared to the ages of your children. Don't expect little ones to sit rock-still for twenty solid minutes of Bible reading. Gear what you do to their interests, their level of understanding, and the length of their attention span.

Second, try different approaches. Experiment. Don't get stuck in a rut, and don't worry if some ideas don't work too well. You can always try something else the next time. But you don't want family worship to get boring or to become the vain, mindless repetition Jesus warned about in Matthew 6:7. And with the variety of helps available today (talk to your pastor or local Christian bookstore owner), there's no reason you should get stuck in a rut.

Third, at least some of the time, let your kids be active participants and not just spectators. Get them involved and worship will be much more meaningful to them now, as well as something that's far more likely to develop into a lifelong habit. Let them read the Scriptures. Have them act out a biblical story, complete with homemade costumes. As they get into the elementary school years and beyond, they can retell a biblical story in their own words, perhaps illustrating with original artwork. Invite them to ask questions about the passage under consideration and how it applies to their lives. (And don't be afraid to answer, "I don't know," as long as you add, "but I'll find out and get back to you as soon as I can.")

Whatever approaches you use, the Bible and family worship experiences need to be a daily part of life, not just a Sunday stopover.

Finally, I have to say to all us husbands and fathers that it's *our* privilege and responsibility to set the spiritual tone in the home. God will hold *us* accountable for how faithfully we've nurtured our families—we can't pass it off to our wives as far as He's concerned. It's our assignment to lead the family in worship. *It's our job to see that everyone's up and ready for church on Sunday*—yes, you read that right. Those of us who have ignored this responsibility or left it to our wives need to get on our knees and ask God's forgiveness, then gently reclaim that role as given in Genesis 18:19, Ephesians 6:4, and many other scriptures.

Disciple

I spent the entire last chapter discussing the importance of the example we set as parents. It's probably the single most important part of guiding our families in this misguided world. But now let me expand on the idea specifically in the area of helping our kids develop a real, personal faith in God.

In his epistles, the apostle Paul several times told believers they should follow his example (see 1 Cor. 4:16; 1 Thess. 1:6; 2 Thess. 3:7, 9). He put it most boldly in 1 Corinthians 11:1: "Be imitators of me, just as I also am of Christ." As daunting as it may seem, we parents should say the same to our children—and then live in such a way as to back it up.

This has all kinds of implications for our daily lives, and I would challenge you to think through just how your example should become more Christlike (with God's help) if it is to help develop that same Christlikeness in your kids.

Discipling our children means more than just leading moral lives. It means spending time with them so they see how we live out the gospel. It means letting them see us in prayer and Bible reading daily, and in Bible study regularly (which implies, of course, that we're doing those things in the first place).

Discipling also means involving our kids in ministry with us. I remember that when I was in my early teens, my father and five or six other men from church would go downtown to preach to passersby on a street corner. Dad would often take me along. I also remember going with him as he preached to prison inmates. As much as possible, I stood by his side while he ministered.

Those experiences played a big part in God's calling on my life and the shaping of my ministry. And not long ago, I found myself talking with my older son, Anthony, about accompanying me in some ministry work. It occurred to me that my father's discipling was being passed to yet another generation.

Another part of discipling is taking advantage of what Josh McDowell calls "teachable moments" when we're with our kids. The idea is to be alert to and make use of natural teaching situations as they arise.

The best of these are when our children come to us with questions. We should always give their questions high priority if at all possible. That means taking a few minutes to set aside what we're doing, look them in the eye, listen carefully, and answer seriously. Kids are never more open to learning than when they've taken the initiative, and they can pay us no higher compliment than to believe we'll listen closely and answer honestly, to the best of our ability.

If what we're doing at the time simply can't be interrupted, we should tell them specifically when we can entertain their questions, and then we should be sure to keep that promise, because that's what it is. (Please understand, too, that I'm talking to myself more than anyone when I give this counsel.)

At other times, an opportunity to make a point will simply present itself. McDowell tells of a time when he was roller skating with his children on a sidewalk at the beach in Los Angeles. All of a sudden, coming up in front of them was a high wall on which all kinds of sexually explicit graffiti had been spray-painted.

Most parents—even non-Christians— would not want their kids to see such a display. They might speed up a little and hope to whiz by before their youngsters noticed the foul words. McDowell, however, saw that as a teachable moment and seized upon it to provide a lesson.

Sitting his children on a bench in front of the wall, he pointed out each word and phrase and explained what it meant. He also described the beauty of sexual love as God created it for husbands and wives, the gift as it is meant to be understood and enjoyed. Then he went on to talk about the nature of sin and how it tries to corrupt the good things God has given us.

In this way, McDowell took a public eyesore and turned it into a teaching tool. What would cause most Christians to turn away in shock and disgust (not without reason), he looked at differently and so was able to use to teach a memorable lesson for God's glory.

A teachable moment with our kids doesn't have to be so dramatic, however. Looking at the night sky together can easily lead to a discussion about the creation and how God knows every star and every hair on our heads. Watching a TV program together can lead to an analysis of the characters' motives and actions from a biblical perspective. Seeing other children cheat in a playground game can prompt a conversation about God's standards and the reasons behind them. *These moments are available to us every day if we're only alert to them.*

Let's keep in mind one other thing about discipling our kids. Namely, the goal isn't just to shape the way they think and believe, but also the way they *live*. We're not concerned only with how much they know, but also with how much they can and are willing to do for the Lord.

Perhaps it will help us to think of discipleship as a spiritual internship. Medical students who want to become surgeons spend years in school learning about all the parts of the body, how they work and how they can be repaired or, these days, replaced. The students learn when and how to cut, and how to sew people back together afterward. Their heads get filled with knowledge.

If those students proposed to perform actual surgery on you or a loved one, however, you'd decline in a second. Why? Regardless of their grades, regardless of how much they know, they're not ready to be turned loose on live people who want to stay that way. They need hands-on, supervised training from experts.

That's the purpose of a surgical internship. The would-be surgeons first go into operating rooms with skilled, experienced doctors, and the neophytes simply *watch*. They learn by observing; the textbooks come to life, in literal flesh and blood.

Only later, at the appropriate time, do the interns pick up scalpels and, remaining under close supervision by skilled surgeons, begin to assist. Later still, when they've demonstrated the necessary knowledge and dexterity, they begin to perform simple, minor procedures. (Actually, as a sage once said, minor surgery is something they do to people you don't care about!)

It takes years to complete a surgical internship—to turn raw information into professional expertise—and with good reason.

In a similar way, the purpose of discipling is to help turn the biblical truths our children learn from us and others into a mature, living, personal faith. It's an internship, a process that takes place over the years, and it works hand in glove with our other parenting efforts (such as prayer, worship, etc.). It's the way in which knowledge gets turned into action and a total lifestyle that pleases and honors God.

Invite Questions

I've referred already to the teaching opportunity presented to us parents when our children ask questions. But young people also need to feel free to question what they've been taught, even by us. Hard questions like "If God is all-powerful and loving, why do innocent people suffer and die?" are going to occur to them naturally, and we need to welcome those queries. When they're asking questions like that, we also need to accept the strong possibility—without being shocked or jumping on our kids—that for a time they will struggle to believe God is indeed all-powerful and loving. If we try to stop them from questioning, they'll never get beyond a faith we've imposed upon them; they'll never develop a personal, living faith in God.

Psychologist Dr. Donald Sloat explains the situation this way: "The evangelical church seems to have completely ignored the role of self-assertion in human development. In fact, anyone who has studied human behavior knows that the key to building a solid person is the self-assertion against constraints that develops the inner sense of being a real person. Parents have known the two-year-old who defiantly yells, 'No! I will do it myself!' This is the child's first step, assertion, so vital to his personhood, and then after the youngster has stated his position, he is willing to 'renounce' and let Mom start the jacket's zipper anyway. But in order to accept the help, the child first had to refuse it.

"Most Christian parents can accept this self-assertion in a two-year-old, but when a youngster reaches adolescence, parents and the church quickly become less understanding. Perhaps this is because teens can get into bigger trouble than the two-year-old who insists on tying his own shoe. The adolescent stage of life is so critical because it is the bridge between childhood, where decisions are made by others, and adulthood, where young people become responsible for themselves. To become independent, autonomous adults, young people usually have to go through the adolescent phase of rebellion, throwing aside what they have been taught in their childhood, questioning their values, and trying new ways of acting."[2]

I suspect the Holy Spirit had that truth in mind when He inspired the writer of this familiar proverb: "Train up a child in the way he should go, even when he is old he will not depart from it" (Prov. 22:6). We train children in the hope and expectation that years later, they'll be walking with the Lord. But in between, especially in adolescence, they may stray from the path for a while.

Think of the story of the prodigal son in Luke 15. When the young man left his father's home with his inheritance, he was definitely in a state of rebellion against the values and faith his father had taught him. But God used his painful experiences while in that state to mature him and draw him back to Himself. When the youth returned home, he was far stronger spiritually—far closer to God and his earthly father—than the "good" brother who had never questioned, never done anything overtly wrong, and never strayed from the family farm.

We all love that story because of the picture it provides of God's forgiveness. But it also illustrates the way God uses our mistakes and our rebellion to train us. Often that's the only way we'll learn—we won't humble ourselves before God until we have no other options. And especially when our children are crossing that bridge called adolescence into adulthood, they need the same kind of freedom to question and to learn from their mistakes that the forgiving father gave his child in Luke 15. While we should all pray that our children don't have to go this route, the reality is that many will only come to true, long-term spiritual commitment after a crisis of rebellion.

Does that mean we have to let our teenagers engage in the kind of debauchery practiced by the young man in Jesus' parable? I have to answer in several ways.

First, the son did not live that way (nor could he have) while at home. Each family must have limitations beyond which the children may not go. Know what your limits are, and make sure your kids know them. Just realize that older, truly rebellious children may choose to leave rather than abide by those rules.

Second, a lot depends on the individual, God-given personality of a particular child. Kids with more-aggressive, dominant types of personalities will naturally rebel more. Others will feel less need to test boundaries, question values, and challenge authority. A book that explores the different basic personality types (such as *The Two Sides of Love*, by Gary Smalley and John Trent) will help us understand which types our children have and what to expect of them.

Third, we can help our adolescent kids to "rebel" more safely and so forestall their feeling a need to rebel in extreme ways. We can not only respond to their questions about the faith, but even initiate conversations using teachable moments. We can give them the freedom to choose their clothes, hairstyles, and music, allowing them to express their individuality and be different from Mom and Dad. If we don't like their choices, we should not dictate changes but discuss *why* we think they could make better selections. We should also make it clear that responsible behavior will lead to more freedom, whereas irresponsible behavior (as opposed to personal preference in things like hairstyle) will result in less. And always, we should bathe them in prayer.

I realize that what I'm suggesting is easier said than done. I also know certain types of music and dress, combined with antisocial behavior, can signal potentially serious problems. Be very concerned about your children's choice of friends. If you think you have cause for apprehension about your children, talk to your youth pastor, pastor, or a Christian counselor.

As a general rule, however, adolescents need the freedom to question, to make choices, and to learn from the consequences. Only that way will they know God and His truth from their own experiences and not just from what they've been taught by others.

In God's Hands

The most tiring and stressful task I know of is being a Christian parent. We love our children. We believe they're gifts from God, and we want to raise them in a fashion that will be honoring to Him. Yet our world is so misguided and so threatens to mislead them that we're tempted to enclose them in a cocoon and never let them out of our sight.

There are many verses in Scripture that directly discuss parenting, but the ones I try to adhere to most don't mention that role specifically. The verses are Proverbs 3:5-6: "Trust in the Lord with all your heart and lean not unto your own understanding. In all your ways acknowledge him and he will direct your path."

Parents, those verses tell us that we're responsible for setting the spiritual and moral tone for our children to follow. We're responsible for seeing that our sons and daughters are raised in homes where love and discipline are consistent; where our children see what we talk about in church lived out in our families. Our example of Christian living should be appealing to them, never boring or guilt-ridden.

In training them, our job is to give our kids the tools to make responsible decisions once they leave home. If we've equipped them well and sent them out with the right set of tools, we have done our job.

Are we going to do this job perfectly? Of course not. But the Lord knows our hearts and is able to overrule our shortcomings and emphasize our strengths.

Will some of our kids end up as prodigals despite our prayers and best efforts? Yes, I've seen it happen many times. Ultimately, we can't decide for our children how they'll live and how they'll choose to relate to God. That's between Him and them.

We can take hope, however, from Jesus' story of the prodigal. When the young man left, all he knew of God and His ways was what his father had taught him. He was a second-generation "believer" with no personal, living faith. But through his experiences, he learned firsthand that God's ways are good and wise. He recognized his need to depend upon God. His natural human pride was broken before the Almighty, and he became genuinely humble, returning to the training he had received at home.

In other words, while he left his earthly father, His heavenly Father *never* left him or stopped training him. And he returned home having made the spiritual journey all our children *must* make in one way or another. He had a living, *personal* faith in the God of his father, one that would sustain him the rest of his days. In the same way, through us and through other people and experiences, our all-wise and loving Father is constantly drawing our children to Himself as well.

They could not be in better hands. Let's just make sure we give Him something to hook onto when He begins the process of reconciling them to Himself.

CHAPTER SEVEN

Can We Talk?

People today benefit from the most advanced information systems ever devised. Folks who died just a hundred years ago would be astounded if they came back to life now and saw the incredible ways we can communicate. Through television and satellites, we can watch what's happening on the other side of the world as it occurs. We can slide a letter into a fax machine in New York and have it appear seconds later in Paris or Tokyo. If a well-known person dies, his or her book-length biography can be in the stores in a month.

We call this communication, but it would be better defined as mere transmission. Communication takes place not just when a message is sent, but only when it is also received, understood, and acted upon. Given that definition, there is very little real communication going on today.

An awful lot of negative communication is getting through, however, and it's driving a young generation into an unprecedented abyss of violence, suicide, and irreverence toward life. Tipper Gore, in her book *Raising PG Kids in an X-Rated Society*, writes, "But in virtually every medium, the communications industry offers increasingly explicit images of sex and violence to younger and younger children. In the course of my work, I've encountered a degree of callousness toward children that I never imagined existed."[1]

The effectiveness of that negative communication, coupled with the scarcity of good communication within families, is a large part of our problem in guiding our loved ones through this misguided world. We've already discussed the influence of our culture, so let's look in this chapter at how we can communicate better with our spouses and children.

Evans's First Law of Family Communication

In my years as a pastor, I've read a number of books and heard countless lectures on family communication. With few exceptions, they've all been excellent. But based on my own experience, both in my family and in counseling, I believe the first law of family communication has to be this: "There is no quality time without quantity of time." I cringe every time I hear parents say that their schedules are really full, so they make a great effort to spend "quality time" with their children.

Think what this idea would look like if transferred to another area of life. What if the Boston Celtics' Larry Bird had said, "I'm pretty good now. I think I'll just spend fifteen minutes practicing my shooting today. It may not be very long, but it will be quality time." That approach would soon have had Mr. Bird warming a bench.

I still remember seeing the film of Larry Bird out on the floor of the Boston Garden, taking practice shots from several marked spots on the court. The stands were empty, and it would be at least an hour before the rest of the team arrived for the game. But Bird knew there's no quality time without investing a large quantity of time.

Unfortunately, while we would tolerate the attitude in no other profession or endeavor— certainly not in professional basketball—we have no trouble shortchanging our parenting and calling it "quality time." Family communication takes work and skill, and you can't develop those skills if you're not present.

In our family, we've found that one of the

best places for family communication is the dining room table. We're all together (now that I make it a top priority to be there), we're relaxed, and we're enjoying a shared meal. It's a great time to review the events of everyone's day.

What about your family? Are your kids around the table? Do they look forward to coming home because their parents will be at dinner tonight? Or are you rarely there?

Part of the work of communication goes back to the fact of different personalities within the family. Because people are unique, they will respond to the same message in different ways. If I correct a strong-willed child in a stern tone of voice, for example, that youngster will probably take it well, either obeying because of the sternness or feeling free to ignore me!

A sensitive child, on the other hand, might be crushed emotionally by the same tone of voice. The sternness is interpreted as an overwhelming personal attack.

Clearly, I need to know my children's (and my wife's) personalities so I'll understand how to communicate effectively with each one without hurting anyone. And how do I learn their personalities? How do I discover the best ways to communicate with them? It takes time spent with them—there's just no other way.

Family Communication: The Investment

In his book *What Wives Wish Their Husbands Knew about Women*, Dr. James Dobson wrote, "I have concluded that the accumulation of wealth, even if I could achieve it, is an insufficient reason for living. When I reach the end of my days, a moment or two from now, I must look backward on something more meaningful than the pursuit of houses and land and machines and stocks and bonds. Nor is fame of any lasting benefit. I will consider my earthly existence to have been wasted unless I can recall a loving family, a consistent investment in the lives of people, and an earnest attempt to serve the God who made me. Nothing else makes much sense, and certainly nothing else is worthy of my agitation. How about you?"[2]

That "consistent investment in the lives of people" is a good way to look at the effort needed to achieve effective family communication. How often I've walked into an immaculate and very expensive home and felt as though I were walking into a crypt! The parents were social and business climbers and didn't have the time to be with their children, who had all headed down different roads of destruction. Mom and Dad had a mistaken idea of what it meant to provide security.

They were investing their lives in the wrong things.

Put simply: Making an investment in your family may cut back some of the profits. It may mean letting someone else in the office land that big client. In my case, it means saying no to some programs that could help stimulate the growth of our church and national ministry.

The Nuts and Bolts

We've talked about why you need to communicate in your family and what it will cost. Now let's get down to the ins and outs of communication—how you send messages and how you receive them.

In all communication, there are three parts. The *encoder* is the person who wants to say something. The *message* is what's actually said. It's supposed to convey the encoder's intended information and emotion, but it has a life of its own and is easily misinterpreted. The *decoder* receives and deciphers the message to make sense of it.

If the decoder doesn't understand what was received, no matter how clear we (the encoder) thought we were, we may have to repeat ourselves. If our message is still not understood, we may wind up saying something intelligent such as, "Are you stupid or something? Can't you understand English?" We often say these things, or polite equivalents, to our spouses, our brothers and sisters in Christ, and even our children.

Most marital problems boil down to poor communication. When a couple tell me about how they fight all the time, they're saying they don't communicate. When a wife says, "He doesn't understand me," she's saying that who she is and what she says are not getting through to her husband.

I recall a number of times listening to parents give instructions to children that I had trouble understanding myself. Yet when those kids acted as though they hadn't understood the message, the parents said, "Are you dumb? Don't you understand me?" Aside from being insensitive and damaging to a child's self-esteem, such remarks should make us wonder who really is the ignorant party.

Mom and Dad, if you give an instruction to a child and that youngster sends you back a bewildered look, maybe it's not the child who has the communication problem.

Principle 1: Be Honest

Ephesians 4 contains some excellent counsel regarding communications. The first principle found there states: "Therefore, laying aside falsehood, speak truth, each one of you, with his neighbor, for we are members of one another" (v. 25).

The first principle of communication is that we need to be honest. One reason families are breaking apart is the lack of honesty and a consequent lack of trust. People are afraid to tell each other what they really think and feel.

For a simple example, think back to when you and your spouse were dating. Did you ever lie to make the other person happy? Most of us did. The scenario goes something like this: She loves opera—lives it and breathes it. He, on the other hand, can think of nothing he would rather do less than go to an opera.

What does he tell her, however? Does he admit his passion is baseball and he despises opera? No, he says, "Isn't that a coincidence? How did you know I love opera? We'll have to go see one real soon." They do, too, and he pretends to be thrilled.

Later, when he expresses some enthusiasm for baseball, which she hates, what does she say? She lies and claims she loves it just to accommodate him.

The problem comes when those two people get married. They figure, *Now I've hooked him (or her). I don't need to lie anymore.* The next time she suggests they go to an opera, he answers, "I don't like opera. I never liked opera. Who wants to go see a bunch of overweight people sing in a language no one understands?"

The next time he wants to go to a ball game, she responds, "Baseball is a bunch of sweaty men getting dirty and chewing tobacco while they try to hit a ball over a fence with a stick. Are you crazy? I just went before to make you happy."

The truth will eventually come out, and when it does, the foundation of the relationship will be shaken. The trust level will go down. Although the example I gave did not involve an earthshaking incident, it didn't have to. Once our spouses or children see that we'll lie about small matters, their trust in us on more important matters will begin to erode as well. A family's communication will be clouded in suspicion.

Besides hiding what we really think, we also hide our emotions. A friend of mine tells of a husband who noticed that his wife wasn't paying any attention as he talked. He asked her if she was upset, and she said no. Then he saw her getting flushed, and beads of perspiration broke out on her forehead. He asked her again if she was upset. She winced and said no. But her unexpressed emotion continued to build up until one day, without warning, it exploded.

A lot of families are slowly ticking time bombs. Everyone is trying to keep the peace at all costs; when we get angry, we don't dare show it. While it may present a nice, squeaky clean exterior to the world, the family is being poisoned on the inside.

Principle 2: Be Angry and Do Not Sin

"Be angry, and yet do not sin; do not let the sun go down on your anger" (Eph. 4:26).

Take a moment to understand the flow of that statement. It puts to rest a lie (albeit a well-intended lie) that many of us heard as we were growing up in the church—that it's sinful to get upset or angry. All we were told of this verse was "Do not sin."

Because of that misinterpretation, many of us held back, even when our anger was justified. And because we didn't get angry, we built up deep resentments that would come to the surface months—sometimes years—later. We exploded at our friends, spouse, parents, and children, and we didn't know why. We filled a huge storehouse of bitterness.

Scripture records one occasion on which Jesus got extremely angry. He took a whip and drove the money changers out of the temple. He got physically violent with people turning His Father's house into a flea market.

In Ephesians 4:26, Paul told us what we must do with our anger. "Do not let the sun go down on your anger."

By itself, anger isn't necessarily sinful. There may be good cause for it, as in Jesus' case. But anger becomes sin when it's not dealt with promptly. If we get angry at a spouse or our children and don't resolve (or begin to resolve) the conflict right away (implied by the reference to the sun going down), that is sin. If you harbor unresolved anger in your heart for anyone, you are living in sin as well.

Anger is what drives most people to psychiatrists—anger they've repressed for years. When therapists begin to dig this stuff out, they discover rage over issues the people may have thought were resolved long ago. The patients may have been repressing anger toward their parents for decades, all the while lashing out at others to cover up their own anger and hurt.

Sadly, the seeds for unresolved anger are often planted in the church. Tom Skinner says bluntly that "the church is often one of the biggest fakes going." Instead of coming to church to be real, which is what we should do and the only way the Body of Christ can ever help us, we fake our communication and put up a facade, even if we're dying inside. We act as if nothing's wrong in the very place where those wrongs should be addressed.

But we've trained ourselves. Church is the place where we look our best, even when God knows better. Church needs to be the place where we can say honestly, "I need to tell my brothers and sisters about some pain I'm going through, because I need some support."

When Paul told us not to let the sun go down on our anger, he didn't intend to impose some burdensome rule on us. He wrote those words so that we could open the lines of communication and restore some emotional health to our lives. The verse is not deeply insightful; it is simply good, common sense.

Take the verse literally when it's within your power to do so. Settle conflicts with your spouse or your children before the end of each day.

If a member of your family is angry at you, ask what behavior or words set it off. If you're the one who's angry, tell the person why; don't make your spouse or child guess. It won't always be a pleasant conversation, and the resolution may not always be to your liking, but if you get to the root of the problem right away, you will prevent unnecessary seeds of bitterness and resentment from being stored up and exploded later at unexpected moments.

If you reach an impasse, you can never lose by accepting the blame regardless of who's "right." Then there's nothing left to fight about, so you can get on with rebuilding the relationship. That's exactly what Jesus did when He took the blame for our sins on the cross even though He Himself was sinless (see 2 Cor. 5:21)—so we could have a relationship with Him.

Sometimes It's All in Your Head

While some of our anger is justified, a lot of it has little basis in reality or fairness. Many times, if we really get honest with ourselves, we'll find that the root problem is an overblown ego or unrealistic expectations.

We often get mad at loved ones, for example, when they can't seem to read our minds. Rather than just coming right out and asking for something, we get steamed and think, *If they really cared about me, they would know what I want. After all these years, they should know me. I shouldn't have to ask them.*

Another reason for anger in families is what I call the "poor me" syndrome. This syndrome is based on self-pity, one of life's most useless emotions.

In my home and in others, from what I've heard, the syndrome works something like this: I come home after a bad day at the office. Nothing has gone my way. The deacon board dumped on me. I was voted down on three proposals, and two couples who came to me for counseling said my advice did them no good.

As a result, I bring home a real "attitude." I walk in the door and radiate those oppressive vibrations that say, "Don't even think about talking to me. Don't ask me anything, because I might get angry. If you do say something, I deserve to get angry, because I've had a *bad* day." I require my family to read my mind and decide what will and won't make me upset. I get to be God for the evening.

That kind of anger cuts off communication completely. It needs to be dealt with right away, and here's one way to do it: Simply say, "You must be upset about something, and I understand that. But you're not going to ruin this family's evening with your attitude. We'll talk this out later, when the kids are in bed, and then you and I are not going to bed ourselves until this is resolved. In the meantime, try to be civil."

I don't know about you, but I enjoy my sleep. I also realize it's extremely unhealthy to keep poisonous attitudes and resentments bottled up overnight. The roots of bitterness will only be deeper in the morning—and Lois won't let me go to sleep anyway.

Principle 3: When Communication Is In, Satan Is Out

"Do not give the devil an opportunity" (Eph. 4:27). If I were to announce Satan's plan for your family, it would be simple: Divide and conquer, destroy it utterly. His plan is to make sure your family is torn apart.

Satan is a schemer. He connives and is always trying to bring something against you. He is looking for an opportunity to slip into your marriage and ruin it. And one way he can do that is to cut off family communication by making sure husband, wife, and children are so busy running in separate directions that they don't have time to talk with one another.

A good way to thwart this plan is to covenant together as a family that you will be together at the end of the day, no matter how busy the day has been. Decide that every evening you will review your day with one another; make sure your disagreements are settled; make sure you are right in your relationship with each other and with the Lord.

You may come back to me and say, "Wait a minute. I've got a busy schedule. In the evening I have all sorts of other things to do. I've got to see the news and catch up on what's happening in the world."

My response is, "Friend, if you and your

family don't get together for a few minutes on a regular basis, you aren't going to have any world to come home to."

Don't just spend those minutes each evening complaining, either. As a pastor, I know that if the only time you want to meet with me is when you have a problem, we're not communicating with one another. All we're doing is working through the negative stuff.

The same thing applies in a family. Don't just get together when there are problems and complaints. Enjoy those times when all that's on your minds are compliments, praises, and good memories. Celebrate! The devil's foothold in your family will begin to slip if you do.

Principle 4: Speak to Edify

"Let no unwholesome word proceed from your mouth, but only such a word as is good for edification according to the need of the moment, that it may give grace to those who hear" (Eph. 4:29).

That's a straightforward, common-sense communication principle. Don't talk trash or spread gossip about anyone. Only talk about those things that will lift somebody. Make sure that good comes to those who hear you (Evans paraphrase).

We love to put other people down, don't we? We criticize someone loud and long and think that makes us look real good. If the truth be known, however, there is really only one reason we say unwholesome words about friends and family. Historian Will Durant put it well when he wrote, "To speak ill of others is a dishonest way of praising yourself."

I want you to try an experiment for one week with your family. During that time, don't say anything to your spouse or children unless it's wholesome and will contribute to their personal and spiritual growth. For example, instead of asking, "Why isn't dinner ready yet?" a husband might try, "Can I help you with dinner, Honey?" That way he becomes part of the solution and not another part of the problem.

You may say, "That won't be hard."

It won't? I think you'll be surprised, as you become more conscious of your everyday speech, at how precious little positive communication comes from between your lips.

You'll make mistakes. I know that. But after a while, you'll begin to reap the benefits. Whereas now, when you say something nice, your spouse and children may wonder what you want from them, you'll soon find the barriers breaking down when they realize you're sincere. As the bitterness and rage begin to disappear from your communication, the forgiveness and compassion needed to hold a family together will start to flow.

Principle 5: Listen

Much has been written and preached in recent years about the need to listen, but I have to mention it here because it's so important. Most of us are still lousy listeners. When someone else is talking, even if it's directly to us, our minds are on something entirely different—like what we want to do next or what we're going to have for lunch in half an hour. If we're more involved in the conversation, we're thinking about what we want to say when next we interrupt.

It's so simple that it seems almost silly to say it, but I feel I must make the point: If we're not listening to what someone else is saying to us, we'll *never* get the message clearly.

We have to work at listening. If our kids come to us with a question while we're reading the paper, we have to put it down long enough to make eye contact, listen closely, and respond. If we're watching TV, we have to look away from it. Eye contact is crucial, and it doesn't hurt to get down to a child's level to make it.

If we're told something and we don't

understand completely, let's not be too proud to ask for clarification. We can also repeat what someone said and ask the person to confirm that we've understood properly. This is all a part of good listening, and without it real communication is impossible.

There's no shortcut to communicating love to our children and our mates. It takes work. It takes being kind to our kids when we're not feeling kind but know they're asking for love and attention. It takes being patient with our spouses when what we really want is to get our own way. It takes forgiving our children seventy times seven times and welcoming them back when they return from the path of the prodigal.

It takes talking.

It takes listening.

And it takes a powerful Christ to see us through.

CHAPTER EIGHT

Your Home: Dry Ground in a Muddy World

When you think back on some of your fondest memories, what pictures come to mind? If you're anything like me, a lot of those memories center on your home. We think of Mom greeting us after school, of playing ball with the other kids in the neighborhood, and of Mom or Dad trying to pry us out of bed in the morning to get ready for school.

The most special times I remember, however, are those times when the whole family was together at church, on a family outing, or just cleaning up the house or the yard together. Some people would call those events ordinary, but I call them special.

Home was my refuge. I felt safe there. I could let down my guard, be myself, and know that I'd still be loved.

I've been accused of waxing a bit nostalgic from time to time. I've been told not to live so much in the past. But given my line of work, it often helps to restore my hope if I remember how family life was in my childhood and dream of how it could be for other families. In my role as a pastor, I'm confronted with heartbreak and family dissolution daily. And though I see occasional signs of hope, they are less frequent with each passing day.

Some folks tell me I'm just imagining how good things were in the past as far as families are concerned. They tell me that maybe there are a few more divorces today, but all that's really happened is that our communication systems are better and we find out about things a lot sooner.

For a time I thought, *Well, maybe it is just me. Maybe we're just hearing the bad news quicker these days.*

After talking with a man about my same age a while back, however, I began to see that I'm not really as far gone as some people would have me think. In the course of our conversation, this other man began to lament about the past.

"You know, I'm almost forty years old," he said. "I haven't chosen to get married yet, and maybe that's because I'm a bit apprehensive about things. Everywhere I look, I see families splitting up. It's getting so it's a lot easier to find a family that's fallen apart than one that's together.

"Just recently, I started thinking about the neighborhood I grew up in. In my mind, I started naming off the families that lived on my block. Then I started naming families that lived a block or two away. You know, I couldn't even think of a family that had split up. Some families had problems, including ours, but we were all still together. It seems as though the kids in the neighborhood had a kind of floating party going on. We'd go from yard to yard, house to house. It just seems that there was a spirit of welcome all around. But to tell you the truth, I honestly can't remember a family where Mom and Dad weren't together.

"Today, I just have to look around and shake my head. I must admit that I do want to get married and have a family, but I don't know. Who would want to bring up kids in this kind of world?"

I'm sure many people could echo that man's comments. He's scared, and I don't blame him. It seems as though each day that passes brings more and more difficulty for the family.

Hope Begins with You

I believe there really is hope for the family, however, or I wouldn't have written this book. And I believe there's a ministry we can have as parents that can go a long way toward realizing that hope not only for our own families, but also for the families of our neighbors and our children's friends. That's what I want to talk about in this chapter.

The word picture I've been using to describe our job is guiding our families through a misguided world. But let me change the metaphor here to say we live in a muddy world. Values and beliefs and roles are no longer clean and clear. They've become muddied. And every time you step in mud, it sticks to your shoes, and you track it everywhere you go, befouling every part of your world. It's also slippery and easy to fall down in, and then you're really a mess.

What children need is high, dry ground on which to stand—a place that's safe and clean, with sure footing, and from which they can see the world clearly. Our homes can be such places if we'll work at it.

Here's what I mean. Human beings are social creatures. Although some of us like solitude more than others, most of us like to do things with other people. That's certainly true of children. Young kids like to have playmates, usually from the neighborhood. As children get older, they and their friends go from playing with toys together to playing sports. Later still, they do homework together, talk, and play computer or video games.

They need a place to do all these things. And rather than have them off at the nearest shopping mall or who knows where, why not have them and their friends right there in our own homes? Why not create a safe haven, a patch of dry ground, under our own roofs? There are several good reasons for doing that.

First, what better way to know our kids are safe and not getting into trouble? Kids can *always* find ways to get into trouble, I know— I'm not naive about that—and we have to respect their privacy when they shut their bedroom doors (except in extreme situations, such as having good reason to believe they're using drugs in there). But they're far less likely to get into trouble at home than they are at a lot of other places where they might otherwise hang out. And if we create the right atmosphere (more about that shortly), the kids won't be holed up behind closed doors all the time anyway.

Second, having our children bring their friends home means we get to know those friends a lot better than we normally would. The older our kids get, the more important their choice of friends becomes, because those friends exert an ever greater influence on them. Therefore, we *need* to know who our children are spending time with, and having the friends in our homes makes the learning process relatively easy.

Third, we can have a positive Christian impact on those children. By our welcome, acceptance, love, and example, we can build them up and point them to the Lord. As the opportunity arises, we can even present the gospel directly. That's how we provide the patch of dry ground that all kids need.

If your neighborhood is typical, most of the children are living in a single-parent home or a home where both parents have outside jobs. Many of those children are latchkey kids. You probably don't realize how many of your children's friends go home from school every day to an empty house. I don't care what kind of front a child puts up, it's difficult to go back to an empty home every afternoon.

I know people who have developed a full-fledged ministry to neighborhood latchkey kids almost by accident. Their homes have become afternoon havens. In addition to providing a place to go for a few hours every afternoon, the moms who open their homes are giving a powerful witness to the true meaning of the gospel. Their acts of kindness and generosity speak louder than any ten sermons.

My Poor House!

Those are some good reasons for building the kinds of homes where our children will feel encouraged to bring their friends and where their friends will always feel welcome. But I can hear some of you moms saying about now, "Oh, that's just what I need, a lot of kids traipsing through the house all the time. How will we ever get anything done? Besides that, the place will always be torn apart!"

I understand your concerns; they're legitimate. So let's see if I can ease your mind a little.

Realize first that I'm not talking about a twenty-four-hour-a-day free-for-all. I'm simply talking about a place where your children and their friends will feel comfortable. Since you're the parent, you regulate the hours. There's no need to install a revolving door at the front of your home.

Don't be afraid to enforce your normal family rules, either, about things like how much roughhousing is permitted indoors, where food may be eaten, what language is acceptable, and so on. Kids who visit need to know that you run a home that has set up certain standards and intends to live by them. There's no need to be an ogre about any of this, but you do need to make clear what will and will not be tolerated. Let kids be kids, and make them feel welcome, but also mark off the boundaries.

In some cases, visiting children may get a bit upset about your guidelines. I've found, however, that deep down, most of these kids respect parents who set up standards. A lot of your children's friends will come from homes where the rules are clear. But others will come from homes where the standards are loose or there are no standards at all. Though some of those kids may balk at first, most of them will end up admiring you.

An even more basic issue has to do with your priorities. As you consider the possibility of making your home into a haven for children, a place where your kids and their friends *want* to come, what pictures come to mind? Are you excited about the potential ministry, or are your thoughts all about spilled soft drinks and dirty bathrooms?

I'm reminded of a story told by a former major league baseball superstar. One day when he was a boy, he and his friends and his father were out in their yard playing ball. They played there regularly, and the grass had really taken a beating as a result. It didn't look very good anymore unless you were a child looking for a nice place to play baseball.

On this particular day, as the kids and the man were playing in the yard and having a great time, the boy's mother leaned out one of the windows and called to the father,

"Can't you guys find someplace else to play? You're killing the grass."

The man looked at his wife and answered, "Honey, we aren't raising grass. We're raising kids!"

I believe that father had his priorities in better order than the mother. That doesn't mean her concern was invalid, and I'm not saying you have to be prepared to sacrifice your lawn to make kids feel welcome. Perhaps a compromise could have been found (e.g., play at a neighbor's house every so often). But the spiritual and emotional health of children is clearly more important than the health of grass, and we all need to decide what our highest priorities are.

Making Kids Feel Welcome

By now, I hope you're receptive to the idea of opening your home informally to children. So let's turn our attention to practical ways to make them feel welcome.

Kids are always hungry, and they'll love you if you have something for them to eat. My wife, Lois, has a real gift of hospitality, and our kids' friends know that whenever they come over, she'll feed them something good. It may be milk and cookies, a sandwich, or some barbecue. If the children are there at dinnertime, she'll invite them to stay and join us (making sure they call their parents for permission).

Another thing we do that kids seem to appreciate is to make them a part of our normal activities. (This also gets at the concern of "How will we ever get anything done?") If I have some errands to run, I invite our child and the friends to join me. If Lois is going to the mall, she'll take them along. Our daughters' friends often help them do the dishes. And our sons' friends will help them clean up the garage or do whatever other chore they have to finish. This isn't exciting stuff, but these activities make our guests feel like part of the family.

Something both we (Lois and I) and the kids enjoy is for us to occasionally give them our undivided time and attention. Almost every time our sons have friends over, for example, I go out and play basketball with them. (I usually win, too!) In fact, they get upset when I don't play. Sometimes I set up races for them or serve as all-time quarterback (quarterback for both sides) in a football game.

We also take time to talk with the kids and find out about their families, schools, and hobbies. Our daughter Chrystal's college roommate has practically become another member of our family as we've gotten to know her during her visits.

We often let our children's friends stay

over for the night. They don't require a guest room; the floor is just fine. Supermom Lois always has a big breakfast for them the next morning. About once a month, our kids bring their friends over to watch an approved video and munch popcorn. In addition, our children and their friends know they're always welcome at our house to work on things like school science projects and informal youth choir rehearsals.

The Spiritual Side

How do we handle the spiritual side of this ministry? We try to make it as natural as possible, just as it's a natural part of our family life.

When it's prayer time in our home, it's prayer time for everyone who's there. We all join hands and talk to the Lord (though we would never pressure guests to participate verbally). If it's time for family devotions, our friends get to hear the Scripture read and then discussed.

Lois and I also try to turn discussions with our children and their friends to spiritual matters. It's easy to do, as kids are eager to talk about topics like music, school, and the opposite sex. We simply offer them a biblical perspective on those subjects (without being preachy) and ask them to give it serious consideration. From our example, our children are learning to do this, too.

We also encourage our kids to be bold in witnessing to their friends. It's one thing for peers to know they don't smoke, drink, do drugs, or sleep around because they're Christians. It's quite another to give positive witness for Christ and confront friends regarding their own standing before the Lord. This is intimidating, and we're patiently training our kids, but it's also necessary in light of the Great Commission Jesus gave all His children.

"Won't some children or their parents be offended if you witness to them?" you ask. That's always a possibility. We try to be sensitive in how, when, and where we share our faith, and we certainly don't plan to offend anyone. But our relationship to God through Christ is the central reality of the Evans home, so how can we keep silent about it? Parents whose children visit us need to know we're Christians; if they don't know it at first, they soon find out—again, not in an overbearing way, but just as a natural part of our daily life as a family.

You Can Do It

Nothing I've talked about in this chapter requires that you have a big home or a lot of money. But making kids feel welcome does require a lot of desire and a fair measure of flexibility. It does require prayer. There are no complicated formulas or twenty-point plans.

But in an age when we see the family crumbling around us, isn't it exciting to think about the influence one family can have on a lot of kids and, by extension, their families? Choosing to make our homes dry ground in a muddy world will bless not only our own children, but many other families as well. Just one Christian family, dedicated to having a home that serves Christ by serving others, can have tremendous impact. If only a few families in every town catch the vision, we can help turn around a hurting world.

CHAPTER NINE

How Your Church Can Help

One of the most beautiful, encouraging verses in the whole Bible is Hebrews 13:5: "For He Himself has said, 'I will never desert you, nor will I ever forsake you.'" Many times, especially in difficult circumstances when all other evidence seemed to suggest God was nowhere to be found, I've drawn comfort and reassurance from that promise.

I've observed, however, that Christians usually think of the presence God promised as being only in the person of the Holy Spirit. We know He indwells us, and sometimes we sense His nearness in special ways. That's great, but that's not the only way God fulfills His promise—not if the church is functioning the way it's supposed to.

In scriptures like Galatians 6:2, 9-10, Acts

2:42-47, and many others we could list, believers are exhorted to help one another, to teach one another, to bear one another's burdens. And besides the work of evangelism and Bible teaching, what greater mission can the church undertake—especially in this misguided age—than to strengthen and support its families?

In other words, as we parents seek to guide our families according to God's will in an antagonistic culture, we should not be standing alone. Our local churches should be standing with us and providing all kinds of help. When they do, our hands are greatly strengthened.

The purpose of this chapter is to explore specifically what sorts of assistance the church can provide. Then, from a pastor's perspective, I'll suggest ways you can work with your church leadership to make your church more family-supportive.

1. Develop Strong Children's Programs

It has become a stereotype that on Sunday mornings, Mom and Dad have to drag the kids out of bed and practically whip them to make them get ready for church. It's almost as if children view going to church on a par with going to the dentist to have teeth drilled without Novocaine. That's a tragedy! Our children should look forward to going to church because of all the fun, interesting programs and loving people waiting there for them. And those programs and workers should be helping parents train their kids in the nurture and admonition of the Lord.

A good children's program is also vital for another reason. When I was growing up in Baltimore, I didn't worry much about being kidnaped, molested, or arbitrarily harmed. While those things happened, they weren't rampant and tended to be restricted to the late-night hours in the most isolated places.

Not anymore. One of the tragic consequences of the removal of God from our culture is that evil people feel less compelled to hide or limit their wickedness. As a result, parents must watch their children like hawks, analyzing every playmate, scrutinizing every program, and approving every activity. This has turned parenting into a policing job of great magnitude.

Unfortunate as that is, however, it presents the church with a tremendous opportunity. By developing well-supervised, fun-filled programs, it can provide the safe and secure environment parents want for their children. That's not only good for the parents who are church members, but it's also a terrific drawing card for non-Christian parents who want the same benefits for their kids.

In other words, a good children's program is an extremely effective way to draw whole families into the church, where they can hear the gospel. Especially in this day and age, it can be one of our best evangelistic tools.

One of our popular children's activities at Oak Cliff Bible Fellowship is the annual Halloween outing. Our goal is to provide an edifying, safe alternative to the usual ways the holiday is celebrated. In addition to the dubious spiritual background of Halloween, trick or treating has become a matter of life and death.

Our approach is to turn that day from a time of celebrating Satan to a time of celebrating God—without losing any of the fun. We call it All Saints Eve. The children dress up as biblical characters rather than ghosts or goblins. Hundreds of kids come with their parents to an exciting evening of games and crafts. And since we purchase the candy, the parents don't have to worry about the recent evil of candy laced with drugs and razor blades.

One of the best things we did for our children was to establish a midweek program just for them. The one we use is called AWANA (Approved Workmen Are Not Ashamed); Pioneer Clubs is another excellent program. It features Bible verse contests, Scripture lessons, and all kinds of fun time.

The kids can't wait to come to AWANA on Wednesday night. My younger son, Jonathan, would rather study his AWANA book than look at TV, just so he can be sure to earn his prize. Children literally drag their parents to church that night.

Sports are also an important outlet for kids. We offer baseball and basketball teams, and lots of youngsters take part.

Special emphasis needs to be given to programs for junior high and high school students. They're the ones for whom negative peer pressure is the greatest danger; they're the ones who can get into the greatest trouble if they don't have the right kind of influences in their lives.

Such programs need to include solid Bible study, frank discussion of kids' questions and concerns, and a warm atmosphere of love and acceptance. Recreational activities should cater to the kids' interests. One youth group I know is big on camping; another does a lot of water sports; yet another is really into bowling.

Ministry to others ought to be another vital part of the youth program. This can involve service to the poor, the sick, the elderly, or some kind of evangelistic outreach. The specific service isn't as important as the principle that young people need more than to be entertained. Each year, our church sponsors a youth mission trip to some third-world country so our kids can help some needy folks and also develop a heart for ministry.

The bottom line to all this, as they say in business, is that my kids would rather be at church than at home. They have so much fun there and so many good friends that church has become a sort of home away from home. Lois and I couldn't be happier.

2. Offer Child Care at Church Services and Day Care During the Week

As much as parents love their children, they need occasional breaks from them. In addition, parents usually find it much easier to concentrate on worship in a church service if they're not having to look after their young kids. And the little ones themselves have a hard time behaving for the full length of a worship service.

For all these reasons, a church that wants to help its families will provide quality children's ministry during worship services and for as many other adult programs as appropriate. That way, parents know the children are in good hands, and Mom and Dad can be fully involved in their activities. The kids will be happier, too. An added benefit is that child care is another drawing card for non-Christian parents.

A serious, related concern facing the American family today is the issue of day care for working parents. Like it or not, the issue is here to stay, and the church had better wake up and begin to address it. The reality is that more and more mothers will be joining the work force just to make ends meet. Add to this the astronomical growth of single-parent families, and it becomes clear that the issue is not "Should there be day care?" but rather "Who's the best at providing it?"

The answer is also crystal clear. Outside the extended family, the church is the best option for quality child care while parents are at work. Why? Because if a church is truly Christian, it will understand like no other what it means to be a family, since that's exactly what a true church is supposed to be. The church will also respect the position of the parents as the primary authority in children's lives, a role that is being greatly infringed upon by our godless society.

Because of all the recent day-care scandals, parents are desperate to find centers that are ethically sound, morally responsible, and affordable, and that embody the precepts and values they themselves hold dear. The beauty of all this is that day care becomes yet another wonderful opportunity for the evangelization of children as well as parents.

Most churches already have the basic facilities needed for a day-care center. The other main ingredients are some staff who have a vision for day-care ministry and perhaps some remodeling (ask local officials about fire codes, licensing, and so on). And such a ministry will even pay its own way in most cases.

In addition to providing day care, many churches should consider starting a full-fledged school so that children, especially during the elementary years, can receive a quality, Christ-centered education. While we shouldn't forsake trying to improve the public schools, we *should* want to offer the children of the community the benefits of a Bible-based education.

3. Give Marital and Parental Training

If the truth be told, couples know much more about falling in love than they do about building a strong marriage. It takes only a few minutes to get married, but it takes a lifetime of work to keep the relationship thriving. Yet the only legal requirements for marriage relate to age and blood tests. That's part of the reason so many marriages fail.

The church can make a big difference here. All of us pastors should require couples to go through premarital counseling before we'll perform a wedding. I don't mean just one thirty-minute session a week before the big day, either. I mean a series of meetings in which the couples explore openly, to the pastor's satisfaction, their views on such things as sex, money management, the number and timing of children, who will do which chores around the house, how they'll spend vacation time, where they'll go at Thanksgiving and Christmas, and so on.

In other words, the pastor needs to help the young lovers cut through the romantic fog to the nitty-gritty issues of daily married life. It's much better for a couple to decide they're not really suited for each other at that stage than for them to enter marriage in haste and regret it afterward at length.

Just as young couples know more about warm fuzzies than they do about how to make a marriage work, so they also know more about making babies than they do about raising them. Far too many parents are simply cloning their own parents in the way they raise their children, with very limited knowledge of God's guidelines for building a strong Christian family.

Like our kids, we're also being slowly but surely led astray by a world that has redefined the meaning of family. On TV, for example, kids talk back and dictate the rules. Parents are portrayed as inept, ineffective leaders whose major role is to be the straight guys for the puns and insults of their children.

Parents, then, need training in how to be parents from God's perspective. And again, what better place for this than the church? Parenting should be a regular topic in adult Sunday school classes and small-group studies. Young, struggling couples can be paired up with wise, older parents whose kids are already raised.

At Oak Cliff, we also have ongoing training for soon-to-be parents, new parents, single parents, and parents with problem children. We have fourteen-week classes, all-day-Saturday seminars, and special parent retreats.

We parents today need all of this kind of help we can get, because we no longer have the support of a culture that at least respects biblical values. So here again is another wonderful opportunity for the church to minister.

4. Provide Christian Counseling

Good training before and after marriage will do a lot to strengthen families. But it will never forestall all problems, and in reality, Christian families are falling apart in droves. They need personalized help to oversee the gluing process to hold them together.

There are problems, however, in getting good Christian counseling. On the one hand, every church is likely to have more need for counseling than the pastor can possibly handle. So families may have to wait or else deal with a worn-out pastor. On the other hand, Christian counselors in private practice, if they're available, often cost more than many people can afford.

What can the church do? I believe the best answer is for the church to train lay counselors who can *walk alongside* those who are in need, comforting them with the comfort wherein they have been comforted (see 2 Cor. 1:3-4). Similarly, older women need to teach younger women about loving their children (see Titus 2:3-4), and older men should teach younger men how to father.

At Oak Cliff, we recently hired a man who has his Ph.D. in counseling. His major job isn't counseling, however, but the developing of a team of lay counselors. He will train them and supervise their work, helping us attain what every body needs, the healing that every joint supplies (see Eph. 4:11-16). He'll also handle the more difficult cases.

I realize, however, that most churches don't have the financial or personnel resources to do what we've done. Yet their people deserve the same quality of love, encouragement, and assistance with their children. So how can those churches help their folks get good counseling when they need it? Let me suggest several possibilities.

First, many churches could bring in a counselor on a contract basis to train lay people to handle simple cases. That way the church body is still involved, the people get good training, and the church doesn't have the expense of an additional staff person.

Second, if professional help is needed, many Christian counselors work on a sliding fee scale. That is, those who can afford it pay the full fee, but those who can't are charged lesser fees in keeping with their income. A pastor should first interview counselors to learn which ones he would feel comfortable referring parishioners to, and next he should ask about their payment policies. That information can then be given to people when referrals are made.

Third, for those who simply can't afford any fee, the church might be able to offer some financial assistance.

Almost every church, however, has someone (usually elderly) who, through experience if not academic training, can offer rich insight into life and relationships. Those folks should be sought out and given opportunity to help their brothers and sisters in the Lord.

5. Furnish Resources Through a Church Library

No church should be without some sort of library filled with materials on the family. There's a multitude of good books, videos, tapes, and magazines available today, yet most Christians never visit a Christian bookstore. Those resources can be made accessible through the church library.

At our church, I highlight two or three books each month that I feel will benefit the family. We can't keep enough in stock, because the people eat them up. They're hungry for good material and just need help in choosing what's best.

Cassette tapes of music and Bible teaching are excellent resources as well, because so many people have tape players in their cars these days and can listen while they drive to and from work.

The church library should also have lots of reading material and tapes for children to stimulate them in their young spiritual growth, and also intellectually. The library might also loan tape players to parishioners who don't have their own.

6. Provide Financial Counseling

Debt is killing American families financially, including many Christian families. In addition, husbands and wives frequently disagree about how the family's money should be spent. The result is that thousands upon thousands of families live under constant tension, and many of them don't survive. Money problems and disagreements, in fact, are the number one cause of divorce.

The church must stop treating money as though it were evil (except, of course, when it comes to tithing!); the apostle Paul said the *love of money* is the root of all sorts of evil. Saving our families includes saving our finances. It means teaching biblical principles of budgeting, financial planning, saving, investing, giving, and so on.

Oak Cliff Bible Fellowship has formed a team of accountants, financial planners, insurance agents, and other professionals to help couples establish budgets. They also help families develop and stick to debt-reduction plans. In addition, anyone who comes to our church for a loan must show a family budget and get financial counseling. All this is done in a context of teaching parents the Bible's perspective on money, and it's all done by volunteers.

Where it's needed, churches can also assist church members in the areas of skill development, job search, and personal investment. Finally, when the parents have their own finances in order and are setting a good example, the church can teach them how to train their children to handle money.

7. Create Family-Centered Worship Experiences

I wrote earlier of how the church should provide child care at worship services, and I believe in the rationale I gave for that. But let me qualify those thoughts a bit at this point. Church events shouldn't *always* separate the family. After all, we want to teach families how to have devotions as *families*. And if handled properly, worship times when the children are sitting beside their parents can be especially meaningful and help build closeness.

At one time I grew concerned about the total lack of family worship at Oak Cliff. Each Sunday, the kids went off to their own programs while their parents were in the worship service. Parents and children all had a good time, but I noticed that when parents and kids were together at other church events, the kids couldn't or wouldn't sit still.

Consequently, we decided to close the children's learning center on all fifth Sundays and have the kids stay with their parents during worship. In addition, the month of December is called our Family Worship Month, and each Sunday the kids participate as part of the general church service. We construct special time in these services to highlight the children. Sometimes I call all the kids forward and we sing "Jesus Loves Me" while the parents listen. Sometimes kids recite Bible verses they've learned. At other times, our puppet ministry ministers to the kids.

Every quarter, we have a church-wide family prayer time. Each family is asked to come to the church for at least an hour of prayer. There is nothing like the beauty of seeing families praise and pray together. This is just another way we take the lead in helping families learn the art of family worship.

Another church I heard about has a special family worship time on Christmas Eve. Tables are set out in the fellowship hall with candles and communion trays on them and kneeling benches on each side. Families go to a table as a group and spend as much time as they like giving thanks to God and sharing with each other the things they appreciate about the Lord and one another. Then they conclude with family communion.

8. Schedule Family-Centered Activities

The church can be a wonderful place to rally the family together for special functions. Our church has regular family fun nights where we offer a variety of games for family participation. On the last Sunday night of each month, families living in the same area gather with the kids for a time of prayer and fellowship. One of the things that evening accomplishes is to remind the nuclear families that they also have an extended spiritual family.

My own cultural heritage stands me in good stead at this point. The black church has always functioned as an extended family. You not only go to church to meet with God, but also to meet with God's family. That's why, in the past, a dinner was often tied to the worship service. It was an all-day affair simply because it was a family affair.

Our individualistic culture has been allowed to rob the church of its biblically based family heritage. This intrusion must be resisted at all costs. The church must set up times to reestablish this family emphasis in support of our struggling nuclear families.

9. Offer Special Help to Single Parents

The church faces a tremendous need—and opportunity—in helping single parents cope with all the added pressures they face. Besides trying to meet the needs of their children alone, they have to stay afloat themselves while burdened with loneliness and often guilt.

Any church that doesn't have or isn't planning to have a significant outreach to singles is not seriously seeking to reach our contemporary world. That world will be made up of 50 percent single parents (70 percent in the black community) by the year 2000.

One of the ways churches can help is to offer their own big brother type of program. (As you may know, the overwhelming majority of single parents are the mothers.) Mature men "adopt" the sons of single women so as to provide them with solid Christian role models. This is what God meant, I believe, when He called Himself a father to the fatherless and a mother to the motherless: He is a father through His surrogate fathers and a mother through His surrogate mothers in the church.

Another way we help is by matching up a "fellowship family" with each single-parent family. Both mother and father are present in these fellowship families, and by spending time with them, the children of single parents get to see a whole family at work and experience fatherly as well as motherly love. They can spend holidays together as well as other planned times.

Churches can organize a monthly evening activity especially for the kids of single parents so the mom or dad can have an evening out and not have to pay a baby-sitter.

We've developed a retreat ministry for single parents as well. Topics discussed on these outings include overcoming divorce, coping with the death of a spouse, disciplining kids as a single parent, dealing with sexual needs, building lasting friendships with your children, the finances of the single parent, and so on. For the children of single parents, we offer discussions concerning the divorce or death of parents, recognizing their responsibilities in the home, dealing with the comments of peers, and adapting to change.

10. Address Family Issues Facing Your Community

Finally, your church can help not only your family, but all the families in your area, by getting involved in the issues facing the community. The church can no longer afford to be silent or passive. It must become proactive.

For example, a church group might address the abortion issue in defense of all unborn children. A politically interested group can analyze the impact of legislation on the family and report to the congregation. Seminars and workshops can be sponsored on helping kids say no to drugs and other issues of community-wide concern. The church can develop its own adoptive and foster-care programs to deal with the problem of unwanted and abused children.

Think of the impact if each church "adopted" a community school. Tutoring programs staffed by church volunteers could be set up for kids struggling academically. Pregnant teens could be cared for by a church family who helped them carry their children to term and stay in school through graduation. In the black community especially, men from the church need to come alongside fatherless black boys to give them a sense of hope for the future.

In these and many other ways, the church can help not only those families within its fellowship, but also those of the entire community. And the evangelistic impact of such efforts could be enormous, to the glory of God.

If your church is too small to do some of these things by itself, you can join with other churches of like faith. More-affluent churches can also share their resources with those who need the help.

Getting an Inactive Church Involved in Family Outreach

I hope some of the suggestions in this chapter sound good to you. You can see how they would help your family and many others. But if your church doesn't already offer such activities and programs, what can you do? Let me offer some ideas.

First, pray about it. I'll say it again: Prayer should always be our first resort, because it's the most powerful thing we can do. Ask God if it's His will for your church to have such a ministry, and ask Him to bring it about if it is. Then ask what part He wants *you* to play in making it happen.

Second, if after prayer and talking to others in the church you think God might want something like that for your fellowship, make an appointment with the pastor to share your vision with him. Before you talk about what's *not* going on in the church, however, be sure to express appreciation for what *is* going well.

Third, make sure you offer specific suggestions as well as your personal willingness to be a part of getting the work started. As a pastor, I've heard my share of people who like to suggest programs but have little interest in helping with the work.

Fourth, follow up your visit with an appreciation letter that summarizes what you understand to be the conclusions of the meeting.

Fifth, act immediately on any open doors so that you fan the coals while they're hot. Keep the pastor or his delegate apprised of the ministry's progress.

If for some reason the church or pastor is not ready for a focused family outreach, continue to pray, avail yourself of the family ministries of other churches, and wait for the next appropriate time to bring the issue back up to church leadership.

When our churches are working to support us as parents and spouses, we're truly never alone.

CHAPTER TEN

You're the One Who Decides What's Right

A popular speaker at Christian men's conferences tells about addressing a weekend retreat not long ago. His topic was father-son relationships, and at one point in his talk, he asked the men how many of their fathers had made a point of discussing girls, dating, and sex with them when they were younger. Out of the one hundred men who were there, how many do you suppose raised their hands?

Three. That's all.

Unfortunately, that pathetic showing of hands doesn't surprise me. You would think most parents would cherish the responsibility of teaching their children in such an important area of life, but I find that's not the case. Many parents, including Christian parents, have handed much of their responsibility over to someone else.

I know there's no realistic way to monitor everything that comes into our children's lives. That's why, throughout this book, I've reiterated the importance of such staples as family worship and good family communication. Children who have clear moral values taught to them at home will have a much easier road when they're on their own.

But besides giving them lots of positive input, we also have to protect them as much as possible from the negative. We need to reclaim our parental responsibility and take the initiative. It's our right, for example, to determine what our kids are taught about sex and other controversial subjects, not the public schools'. *We* should decide, for another example, when our kids are ready to date, not their peers.

This protective aspect of the parental role is kind of like the water filter attached to my kitchen sink. The water coming into my home has already been cleaned by the water department, but a lot of chemicals and dirt still get through. So for the best taste and health in our cooking and drinking water, I installed my own filter on the kitchen tap.

The world has its own "purification systems" for what comes into our homes—network censors screen TV programs, for example, and school boards review sex education curriculums. But those systems are clearly inadequate. They allow far too much dirt to get through. It's up to us parents to act as filters for the health and safety of our families.

Keeping our authority to decide what's right isn't easy, because our misguided culture screams at our children about the joys of sensuality and materialism. The siren calls of hedonism and self-centeredness go out to them from the radio, from books, from magazines, from billboards, from movie screens, from television. Those calls are designed to tell them just one thing: "Listen, your life is humdrum, boring. But if you buy this product or choose this lifestyle, you can make things more exciting."

The two most appealing lures, the ones used to sell everything from shoes to toothpaste, are sex and status (even seven-year-olds know the Reebok Pump is the most "in" athletic shoe at the time of this writing).

Consider the way the liquor and cigarette industries are targeting our children with deadly effectiveness. A *Weekly Reader* survey discovered that the average age at which children begin drinking is twelve. The same survey found that more than 33 percent of nine-year-olds had already experienced some pressure from their peers to drink.[1] A survey conducted in 1988 among high school seniors discovered that 92 percent had used alcohol, and more than half had used illegal drugs such as marijuana or cocaine.

That survey also found that while smoking has declined among the general population, it has remained at a steady level among teenagers. Nineteen percent of those surveyed reported they smoked on a daily basis. The survey results, reported in the February 23, 1990, issue of *American Medical News*, stated: "Virtually all smokers initiate smoking during adolescence, so the implications for morbidity and mortality in these generations are staggering."[2] Evans translation: A lot of kids are going to die from this stuff.

Parents, let's realize what we're up against. The alcohol and tobacco industries spend more than $5 billion a year promoting their products to impressionable minds.

An article in the *Adolescent Counselor* magazine provides an excellent discussion of how those industries target our children's minds. Their advertising is essentially designed to create a myth, not to give information, the article says. It continues: "Advertising does this by linking a product with a quality or attribute. These jeans will make you sexy, this detergent will save your marriage, this car will give you confidence. An article in ADVERTISING AGE (Jan. 27, 1986) on liquor marketing stated that 'product image is probably the most important element in selling liquor. The trick for marketers is to project the right message in their advertisements to motivate those often motionless consumers to march down to the liquor store or bar and exchange their money for a sip of image."'

Those ads appeal to all the things we want—qualities such as "happiness, wealth, prestige, sophistication, success, maturity, athletic ability, virility, creativity, sexual satisfaction, and others—that drug use usually diminishes and destroys."[3]

Forty percent of teenage deaths in this country are caused by automobile accidents, and half those accidents are alcohol-related. The article goes on to say that alcohol is also a contributing factor, if not a major factor, in other causes of death for young people, including suicide and homicide.

In light of those somber facts, I am continually amazed at the number of Christian parents who keep alcohol in the house. Some of the reasons parents give for having it around are ludicrous. "Alcohol is legal, after all, and I don't have a problem controlling how much I drink." "We just use it socially, when friends come over." (That's a reason I hear frequently, as if you need liquor around to be neighborly.)

Remember what I talked about earlier. Children will mimic the behavior of their parents. If your children receive pressure from their peers to drink and also see that Mom and Dad keep a little around the house, don't be surprised if they begin to experiment with alcohol.

Parents, when it comes to the matter of alcohol and tobacco use in our homes, abstinence is the only safe course—abstinence coupled with some instruction about how our children can handle the peer pressure they will undoubtedly face to use those life-threatening substances.

Dr. James Dobson, in his book *Dr. Dobson Answers Your Questions about Raising Children*, gives what I believe is a practical formula for teaching a child how to react to strong peer pressure: "He needs to know in advance how he will handle that moment. Role-play that moment with him, teaching him what to say and do. Your preparation is no guarantee that he will have the courage to stand alone at that crucial time, but his knowledge of peer influence could provide the independence to do what is right."[4]

It's a Question of Authority

What we're dealing with in this chapter is the issue of parental authority—the privilege and responsibility we have to set and enforce the standards in our homes. Think of this authority as drawing the sidelines on a football field. They mark the field of play—the area where the game can continue. Without sidelines, a halfback could run up into the bleachers, past the concession stand, and out into the parking lot to avoid being tackled. The result would be chaos, not a football game. Thus, sidelines don't detract from the game; they're essential to its success.

In the same way, we parents draw sidelines for our children to keep their lives from ending in chaos. We establish standards in our homes and make sure our kids know them. Then, like a referee blowing his whistle and stopping play when the ball carrier runs out of bounds, we tell our kids when they've crossed the line and gone too far. The world is constantly working to blur our sidelines these days—to expand our standards of what is acceptable behavior and confuse our children about how the game of life is played—and our job is to keep those sidelines clear and in force.

Our authority must be exercised in several different arenas. The first is the training of our children. We need to establish sidelines (rules) regarding things like how others are treated, curfews for teens, what kind of language is acceptable, and what kinds of television and movies can be viewed. In enforcing these standards, we must not be inconsistent, letting our kids get away with breaking a rule one day and then enforcing it the next. All that will do is stir up a spirit of rebelliousness and put the seeds of manipulation in their minds. When they discover what rules we're willing to bend and under what conditions, rest assured that they will do everything they can to bring about those conditions.

Children were never meant to drift aimlessly and do as they please. That's why there are parents—to steer them in the right direction so that when they're grown and on their own, they'll know how—and more importantly be willing—to make positive choices.

As I mentioned briefly a couple of chapters ago, children respect authority. Think for a minute about some of the teachers you had going through school. Which do you remember most? Are they the ones who let you do whatever you pleased, turn in assignments late, leave the classroom whenever you felt like it, and who made the tests easy enough that you didn't have to study to do well?

Children think that's the kind of teacher they want. But as adults, we realize that the best teachers—the ones whose names we remember—are the ones who held our feet to the fire, whose word in the classroom was law, and whose tests demanded the best from us. They cared, and they were fair. Their discipline was a mark of their love and concern for us.

Though there may be exceptions to the rule, children generally look back on their parents in much the same way. A young man who was handed money any time he wanted it now finds it hard to manage his spending. Though he may have thought what his folks did was great at the time, he looks back and wishes they had said no more often. On the other hand, a young woman whose parents gave her a certain amount of money each week or month taught her to manage it well. (If she ran out between times, she had to do without.) While it may have been hard for Mom and Dad to say no, this young woman now looks back on her parents with love and a lot of respect.

A word of caution: If you and your spouse disagree about any element of the training and discipline of your children, work out your differences in private so that when you're with your kids, the two of you are presenting a common front. If you're arguing about those things before your children, you've pretty well blown it. The kids will constantly go to the parent who will let them do what they want, undermining respect for the stricter parent and endlessly creating tension and resentment.

At other times, we know what's right and what we should insist upon, but we go against our better judgment because we want to avoid conflict or maybe we're just too tired to deal with it. Children know exactly what buttons to push, and at precisely what times, to get the responses they want. Remember, they're watching us all the time.

I have a formula I try to use in my decision-making at home. I call it the HAT formula. I hold off on decisions if I'm *hungry, angry,* or *tired.* I'm not at my best whenever any of those three conditions prevail—especially being angry or tired. At those times I'm likely to say what I think others want to hear (if I'm tired) or lash out and say something I'll immediately regret (if I'm angry).

There will always be exceptions to the rule, but 99 percent of the time, a decision can be postponed long enough for me to get some rest, cool my temper, or have a bite to eat. It's a mark of maturity to be able to make a snap decision when the situation calls for it, but it's even more mature to say the rest of the time, "Wait a minute. I'm too tired and upset to make that decision right now. Give me a chance to wind down, and then I'll be able to think more clearly."

You Decide What's Right Concerning Sex Education

The second arena where we have to exercise our authority is in controlling the outside influences on our children's values. Nowhere is this clearer than in our kids' sex education. As my opening story in this chapter illustrates, parents have all but abandoned this responsibility to the schools and to other outside agencies like Planned Parenthood. Our sexuality is a gift from God, one of His most precious, but many Christian parents would just as soon go swimming with sharks as talk to their children about it.

Here more than in any other area, however, if we don't do the job, our misguided culture will certainly step in and do it for us, and we won't like the results. We need to get over our own embarrassment—and our natural tendency to condemn and be judgmental—and satisfy our kids' natural and healthy curiosity. As I said at length in chapter 6, we can take advantage of teachable moments as they arise, and we should welcome questions.

If children know that Mom and Dad will take them seriously when they ask pointed questions about sex, they'll be more likely to come to us for honest answers. We can also encourage them to keep us informed about what their peers and others tell them.

Let's be crystal clear about what our kids will be taught if we leave their sex education to the public schools: They'll hear that the question is not whether they should engage in premarital sexual activity but how to do it safely. The condom will be presented as the near-perfect solution to all potential problems. In many curriculums, they'll also be told that the homosexual and lesbian lifestyles are viable alternatives to the man and wife marriage union created and sanctioned by God.

In the public schools, suggesting that sexual abstinence until marriage should be taught is viewed as old-fashioned at best and an illegal intrusion of religious values at worst. When a school district in the state of Washington introduced a curriculum advocating abstinence, it was eventually removed from the schools even though it got good results. Why? "Despite this national acceptance [of the curriculum], the State Superintendent's office ruled that the district violated state regulations because their material acknowledged only the traditional family, gave limited information on contraception, was written from the pro-life perspective, and was presented strictly within the context of marriage."[5]

Who wouldn't be angry? Christians, as well as other concerned parents around the country, are furious that their position on such a sensitive issue is virtually ignored. Yet I contend that the lion's share of the blame for what's going on in the public schools can be laid right at the doorsteps of the church and of individual Christians.

For too long we have viewed sex as a taboo topic, or else we've been too busy or too tired to do our job as parents. The church should also be backing us up in this vital assignment. Dr. Dobson puts it well when he writes, "For families ... which cannot teach the details of human reproduction, there must be outside agencies that will assist them in this important function. It is my firm conviction that the Christian church is in the best position to provide that support for its members, since it is free to teach not only the anatomy and physiology of reproduction, but the morality and responsibility of sex. Unfortunately, most churches are also reluctant to accept the assignment, leaving the public schools as the only remaining resource."[6]

Here's how your church can help. Whether by yourself or with a group of other concerned parents, approach your church leadership. Ask them to offer instruction on the biblical tenets of our sexuality to parents who want to do a better job of teaching their children. Suggest also that biblical information be taught to the church's young people. I'm sure that in your congregation or in your community, there are qualified Christian doctors and counselors who would gladly teach young people and their parents about sex and sexuality.

Violence

Chuck Norris runs through a hail of bullets and is never even grazed. All the while, he's firing two submachine guns that are cutting down the enemy like lawn mowers through grass. Rambo single-handedly overruns an entire Russian outpost in Afghanistan and destroys the high command. When an arrow is shot into his arm, he slowly and agonizingly pulls it out and then cauterizes the wound with a heated knife blade.

Freddy Krueger slashes people into rivers of blood. Jason wears a hockey mask and hacks people, usually attractive young women, to death with an ax.

On prime-time television, people are run over by cars, stabbed, raped, and gunned down in the street every evening before millions of kids. Many of the videos on MTV depict graphic sexual brutalization of women at the hands of dominant and powerful males. Then the late news comes on and gives us the day's real stories of the same kinds of violence.

The net effect of all this violence in the media is that we've become desensitized to violence of any kind. Teenagers who go to horror movies are not horrified at what they see. In fact, many times they actually laugh during the most gruesome scenes. It simply has no effect on them. As adults, when we hear about parents who have abused—even tortured—a child, our dismay lasts for all of about a minute and then is forgotten.

I think of the more than 35 million unborn children who have been killed in their mother's wombs since abortion was legalized. Common methods of abortion include cutting the infant into pieces or burning it to death with a saline solution. It happens so often that we've grown calloused.

Yet we're the ones who determine what's right when talking to our children about the sanctity of life. We have a God-ordained responsibility to make sure that the images coming into our homes and going into our kids' minds are life-giving and life-affirming.

My great fear is that even the Christian community has grown numb. Or maybe we're just tired of fighting the battle. Struggling against government bureaucracies, advertisers, the media, and corporations that don't care can make us weary. It gets tiresome showing up at school board meetings, demanding to have a say in what our children read and hear, and being dismissed as intellectual lightweights because we want our children to learn some truth and solid (i.e., biblical) values. It gets wearying championing the pro-life cause and finding ourselves branded as enemies of women and free expression.

Many Christian parents are still out there fighting the battles and facing ridicule for what they believe. Many others, I'm afraid, have retreated into the comfort of their churches, where they huddle in their groups, talk about topics that have little to do with the spiritual battle we're fighting, and just hope it all will go away.

Still others have become hardened. The violence, the killing, the out-of-control sexual rampage, AIDS, teenage pregnancies, drug and alcohol deaths, and suicides have just become too much. So instead of going crazy, those Christians put up a wall and make sure none of it gets in. It's a natural response. When the mind has been bludgeoned with enough painful stimuli, it eventually over-loads and shuts down to protect itself. My purpose in writing this book, however, is to rally believers everywhere back to the cause of guiding our families through this misguid-ed world. Let's realize we're in a struggle. Let's learn the skills we need. Let's give our families the high priority they deserve in the use of our time and energy. Let's pray for them constantly, and let's also reach out to those around us.

The really good news, of course, is that we don't do any of these things alone. "Those who wait for the Lord will gain new strength," we read in Isaiah 40:31. "They will mount up with wings like eagles, they will run and not get tired, they will walk and not become weary."

Jesus offered in Matthew 11:28-30, "Come to Me, all who are weary and heavy-laden, and I will give you rest. Take My yoke upon you, and learn from Me, for I am gentle and humble in heart; and you shall find rest for your souls. For My yoke is easy, and My load is light."

And the Lord promised in Galatians 6:9, "Let us not lose heart in doing good, for in due time we shall reap if we do not grow weary."

Parents, the battle is ours to win or lose. Sometimes the fight to redeem our culture seems impossible. But God has shown Lois and me, through the Bible and our experience, that as we follow His principles in dependence upon Him, *our families don't have to lose.* There is real hope. "Because greater is He who is in you than he who is in the world" (1 John 4:4).

CHAPTER ELEVEN

Sounds Great, But …

I once read that the best way to get rich is to start with a million dollars. That would make it a lot easier, wouldn't it? There's one major flaw in that strategy, of course, or maybe we should say there are a million flaws. In any event, while there's an ironic grain of truth in that counsel, it's really useless advice.

In writing up to this point, I've tried to be practical and encouraging. I hope I've convinced you that guiding your family in our misguided world doesn't mean you have to become a perfect parent. Nevertheless, I realize that many of you may be saying about now, "All this sounds fine, Tony, but there are some things you don't understand about my situation. I've got some problems with putting your advice into practice."

Without a doubt it's true that there are things I don't know about your unique circumstances. But as long as you're still here with me, let's see if I can't anticipate at least a few of your questions and concerns.

"There's not enough time."

I understand. There are days when I go to the office in the morning, and before I think I've had a chance to get anything done, I look up and find that if I break a few speed limits, I can get home in time for supper.

I would like to tell you that the Evans family worship time and family conference times have taken place on schedule, without interruption, for the past ten years. Unfortunately, if I said that, I would be lying. We make those times a high priority, and we do the best we can to have them. I believe with all my heart that our best is what the Lord asks from us. We get into the trap of trying to do it perfectly, and then we not only fail, but we also do damage to the time we do spend with our children.

Don't become a slave to a schedule, and don't let Satan make you feel guilty when you miss a night. But if you'll give those times a higher priority than distractions like television and reading the newspaper, you'll find you can make time more often than not.

"We've tried family worship, and it didn't work."

It could be that you're trying to make your family worship too much like a church service. First of all, you don't necessarily need to be the one who leads. Family worship often fails because we parents try to run the show. There's no problem at all with putting one of the children in charge.

Look at it this way: In school, your children must sit and pay attention while someone else leads. In church, they sit and listen while the minister leads. In Sunday school, they sit and listen while that teacher leads. Giving them the opportunity to be creative could pay amazing dividends.

Also, check your own attitude about family worship. If you're doing it just because you feel you have to, that attitude will come across to your children. Believe me, they notice when you're not interested or are just going through the motions.

When you do lead family worship, give yourself the freedom to be creative. Don't tie yourself down to what you see in church. We adults can be sticks-in-the-mud sometimes. Worship is a time of joy and celebration that we too often treat as boring ritual. If you need some ideas for creative family worship experiences, I heartily recommend the series of books called *Heritage Builders: Family Night Tool Chest* (Chariot Victor), which you can get through your local Christian bookstore.

"I'm not qualified to teach anyone, including my children. Isn't that what schools and churches are for?"

My response is simple. If you're a parent, you're qualified. If you're a single parent, you're qualified. If you have no diplomas or degrees hanging on your wall, you're still qualified.

You have knowledge no one else has. More than anyone, you know what makes your children tick, what makes them laugh and what makes them hurt. You know, far better than any third party, what's best for them. And no matter what you're told, you abdicate to no one when it comes to your children.

Your kids' spiritual training begins in your home, not in the church building. The church is a wonderful reinforcement for what begins in the home, and you can go there to learn spiritual truths you'll want to pass on to your children, but it does not take the place of your instruction. That's primary.

The type of thinking I mentioned above has tragically led many people to quietly— almost without knowing it—turn over the rearing of their children to outside agencies—some of them even violently anti-Christian. It has happened so quietly, in fact, that we didn't see it until it was too late.

You are qualified. Don't let anyone turn you around on that. You *do* know what's best.

"I'm afraid that if I try to teach my children spiritual things, they'll think I'm a hypocrite."

I hear this from a lot of parents, especially those who have recently become Christians. They look back on their past and fear that because of it, their children won't listen to them now.

As I've said a number of times throughout this book, children are savvy. They know what's going on far more than we might think. I'm not saying that the road will be smooth and that you'll have no problem in helping them grasp your sincerity. You very well might. Remember, you spent quite a bit of time living a life away from God. And you may have misused the trust your children placed in you on a number of occasions. It may take a long time to win back that trust. But it will happen, because once children get wind that the new you is authentic, the trust will come back. It will be tested from time to time, but it will come back.

I've heard the same concern voiced by parents who have been solid Christians for years. They worry that their children will view them as hypocrites, even though nothing major may have ever happened to disqualify them in their kids' eyes.

Even the best parents are far from perfect. If your children want to point out something you're doing wrong, they will. You don't have to worry about waiting for it to happen. If the concern they raise is "Why are you asking me to do something you don't do?" I would listen carefully, then examine my actions carefully. More than likely, there would be something I need to take care of.

Don't wait to be perfect before you begin teaching your children. You'll be waiting a long time. Don't be afraid to ask a child for forgiveness if you've made a mistake, either. Using your mistakes to teach a child forgiveness may be the most important lesson you ever teach.

"My children are almost grown. What's the point in starting any spiritual teaching now?"

In such a case, we have to be realistic, but we can also be hopeful. Above everything else, however, don't beat yourself up for what you feel were your shortcomings as a parent. Don't spend a lot of time asking "What if?" questions. All you'll do is drive yourself crazy trying to repair the past while the present is slipping away.

Maybe your children have already drifted so far into the world that there seems to be no way they will ever make it back. Your own heartache—that gnawing in the innermost reaches of your being that tells you you've failed—keeps you from acting or trying to do anything.

First confess your feelings to God. He already knows them anyway. Second, go talk with some mature Christian parents and explain exactly what you're going through. Don't worry that they won't understand. They will. Confess your failures and your fears to them. I guarantee you will be understood.

And for the child you feel has already drifted too far away to return? Realize that the past is gone and that all you have to deal with is today. Do your best to exert the best influence you can right now, exactly where you are. Each new day, first thing in the morning, offer your child to the Lord completely and allow Him to be responsible for the life of your child that day.

Finally, with the model of the prodigal son in mind, welcome your children home unconditionally should their wanderings in the world come to an end. Like the father in the story, your duty is to forget the past and start fresh, not to haggle and pass judgment on the past when there is rejoicing to do.

Please don't infer that I think any of this is easy. It certainly isn't. Nor do I feel that the results are always ironclad and that children always return. They may not. I'm only 100 percent certain of one thing, and that is that I serve a Lord who holds all power and all strength and who asks me to leave the results of my life and the lives of my children in His hands. I have been asked to give my children the best parenting I can, the Lord knowing I will trip and stumble a thousand times on my journey with them. My children can know, however, that I love the Lord with all I have and that as a father I'm doing the very best I can.

"I'm a single parent, and the burden is too great."

It's true that single parents carry a heavy load, one that at times is overwhelming. But you're a parent and must not abdicate your responsibility.

You can begin to lighten your burden, however, by deciding that you will not try to be Mom *and* Dad but rather the best mom or dad you can be. You may be feeling over-whelmed in part because you're trying to do more than God ever expects of you.

Second, you should identify with a good church that has a dynamic singles program so that you have meaningful relationships with others who are wrestling with the same concerns. Their support, encouragement, and hard-earned insights can be invaluable to you.

Third, you should try to find, preferably through your church, a mother or father figure for your child—someone to fill, at least partially, the parental void. This per-son should be spiritually mature and a solid role model. In my observation, boys especially need this kind of input if their father is missing.

Fourth, you must be strategic in your use of time. When you have free time, being with your child and building that relationship has to be a high priority. Unfortunately, you don't have a partner to share the load. But love your child and embrace the responsibil-ity rather than seeing it as a hindrance to your plans. God will bless you for it.

Finally, develop a relationship with a nuclear family unit so that from time to time, your child can get the experience of being part of an extended family that illustrates all the aspects of Christian family life. Again, the best place to find such an attachment is in your church.

"My kids have already gotten a bad impression of marriage and family because of the mess my marriage is in."

Don't cry over spilled milk. Start where you are, and build from there. If you're in a bad marriage, go to your mate and seek forgiveness for the things you've done to make the marriage bad. Recommit yourself to doing whatever it takes to fix it, including getting professional help if necessary. If you're sincere, there's a much better chance your spouse will respond positively.

When your kids see you and your spouse working hard at healing the wounds in your marriage, they will learn two valuable lessons. First, they'll learn what commitment really means—hanging in there when the going gets tough. Second, they'll learn the beauty and power of forgiveness.

"I've already lost my children's respect."

If you've lost your children's respect, you must earn it back. While losing it is a lot easier than regaining it, it can be done.

First, you must acknowledge that your past words and actions have damaged the relationship, and you must let your kids know that you're committed to fulfilling your parental role from this point on.

Second, you must establish parameters within which your children must operate. Then you must stick with them. Your kids will test you to see if you're for real, and you must hold your ground. This includes the establishment of rewards for obedience and discipline for rebellion.

Once your children know you're serious, they'll begin to take you seriously. That will lead over time to a renewal of respect—but only as long as your actions support rather than contradict your verbal messages.

"How do I find the right kind of heroes to show my children?"

In my own urban community, where the drug pushers and pimps are sometimes seen as heroes, there needs to be a re-education of our children about the great leaders of the past. Kids need to know about the deeds of such people as Harriet Tubman, Sojourner Truth, Frederick Douglass, Richard Allen, and Booker T. Washington. Those heroes stood tall in the face of adversity, trauma, and oppression and still made a difference. So can our kids—in spite of the economic, social, and political crises we face.

Likewise, all children need to hear about such heroes as Martin Luther, William Tyndale, William Wilberforce, Jim Elliot, and Billy Graham.

The Bible, of course, is a great source of spiritual role models. Kids should know all about the faith-filled exploits of Abraham, Joseph, Moses, Ruth, David, Deborah, Gideon, Daniel, Nehemiah, Peter, Paul, Stephen, and a host of others.

Finally, we parents should be vocal critics of the people our children see on TV and hear on the radio. We should not only make clear our opinions of the culture's heroes, but also explain why we feel as we do so our kids will learn the criteria by which to make their own judgments. To do this critiquing, however, we have to be aware of what they're listening to, and we have to analyze what the music or performance actually says. It won't work—nor should it—to condemn something just because it's not our taste in music, drama, or whatever.

My children know exactly how I feel about "the Artist Formerly Known as Prince," 2 Live Crew, and other entertainers whose music fosters ungodliness. On the other, more positive hand, they also know how I feel about Bill Cosby and the values he promotes on his TV show.

I hope that in this chapter I've addressed

the major concerns you've had about implementing the counsel in earlier chapters. It *is* possible to guide our families safely through this misguided world, and we don't have to be superparents. If you have other questions or concerns, however, please talk to your pastor or feel free to write me at The Urban Alternative (address at the back of this book). With God's help, together we can and *will* succeed.

CHAPTER TWELVE

Letters to My Family

Dear Mom and Dad,

Recently you wrote me a letter. In it you shared your gratitude to God for all He has done in my life. You praised Him for taking me as far as He has in ministry.

Well, I'm thankful to God for you, for without you, none of the other things could have happened. Not only were you the vehicle God used to give me physical life, but you were also the vehicle He used to give me spiritual life. Thank you for introducing me to Jesus Christ at a young age.

Every year that I come home to Baltimore, it looks as if more and more devastation has encompassed the old neighborhood. Gone are the good old days. Now the area is full of crime, drugs, poverty, and death. People in the inner city need hope in the midst of despair, and when I see you still on that same block, in that same house, it affirms my ministry. Christ can make all the difference in the world. You live in that environment, but you don't give in to it. Chaos surrounds you, yet it hasn't touched you. Poverty engulfs you, yet God has consistently prepared a table before you in the presence of the enemy. And to see that you're more in love with each other now than you ever were is most certainly a tribute to God's definition of marriage and the truth that God-ordained families can survive any socioeconomic environment.

In that neighborhood you also raised me, taught me about life, gave me a spiritual heritage, and introduced me to ministry. I remember witnessing on the street corners with Dad and going to church as a family every Sunday. I remember the midweek Bible studies in our home and the radio blasting away with gospel preaching and music. It was there, unknown to me at that time, that I was being prepared to do what I'm doing now. I am standing on both of your shoulders, and how tall and strong they are!

If there's one particular lesson I have learned from you, it would be faithfulness. Neither of you has shied away from your responsibilities one iota. You still preach, pray, and sing as heartily as you ever did.

You still have the same standards that were there when I was growing up. I just hope my own children will have half the praise for me that I give God for you.

Dad, I especially want to thank you for your blameless lifestyle and strict discipline. You always lived what you preached. You refused to let me get away with wrong. Even though you had to work long and hard just to make ends meet, you never used that as an excuse to neglect us or God. Thank you for those spankings that I hated so much. Thank you for the time you came to my school when I was suspended for misbehavior, even though you would lose money from work. Thank you for reminding me when I would go out that my name was Evans and I had to live up to it. Thank you for not quitting or leaving us when life was tough and there was no work on the waterfront. In other words, thanks for being a man of God and for not letting me settle for anything else.

Mom, a special thanks also goes to you for always being by Dad's side. You would never allow us to play you against one another. Your ability to take almost nothing and turn it into a gourmet meal still stupefies me. Oh yes, I also remember those double decker sandwiches. The kids at school always used to ask me to get you to make them one. I think you did on occasion. Thank you also for making me do my work. I learned to work hard, and I think that's because I couldn't play football unless I did my school and house work.

I am proud to be called your son, and whatever reward my heavenly Father may give me and to whatever extent He uses me, know for certain that it is your blessing as well. You trained me in the way I should go, and now that I'm older I have not—and by God's grace I will not—depart from it.

My Dearest Lois,

The book of Proverbs says that an excellent wife is hard to find and priceless. I praise God that He allowed me to find a gem such as you. From the first time I saw you in your father's house, I knew there was something special about you. To hear about your love for God, His Word, and His people reaffirmed to me that indeed you were the one for me. The spiritual depth of your mother and father was also a wonderful clue to the kind of person you were. To see the respect and love you had for your parents and the confidence that Ma and Pa Cannings had in you verified that you had received the same magnificent spiritual heritage as I and were the one through whom that legacy should continue.

I have not been disappointed. You lovingly put aside your own career to raise our four children and help get me through seminary. You endured all the inconvenience, frustration, and misunderstanding associated with starting and sustaining a church, at the same time using your gifts to be our first choir director, women's ministry head, and whatever else you were called upon to be. These sacrifices reaffirm that you are indeed God's grace gift to me.

People often ask me, "How does Lois do it all?" I rarely have a response, because I don't know. Yet you're able to balance the preparation of meals with an immaculate house, ministry of hospitality, your music, your continuing education, and your work beside me at church and in our national ministry. In a day when so many women have given up their families for a career or neglected their mates seeking personal gratification, I am so thankful that I don't have that problem.

Few people know of the late hours you must keep to help me. Each Sunday you sit through both morning worship services just to be there to support me, even though the sermon is the same. I realize it's been tough living with this type personality who, because of his job description, often has to tell you to wait while I meet the needs of others. Yet even when you're frustrated by my lack of attention or sensitivity, you're there.

Every time someone compliments me, I think of you. When people speak kindly of our children, I think of you. When people ask me to autograph one of the books I've written, I think of you. When people tell me how my ministry has affected their lives, I think of you. Your presence surrounds every aspect of my life, and your presence in our family is our most powerful asset in protecting our children from the grip of this wicked and perverse world.

As I look forward to the rest of our lives together, I am excited about building an even stronger bond between us. I'm excited about dating you, romancing you, praying with you, and ministering beside you. I'm excited about the prospect of grandchildren and family reunions, about helping other families get and keep what we've been given by God.

Another reason I look forward to the future is that I relish the privilege and responsibility of returning to you all the ministry and sacrifice you've given me. I owe you not because you've ever billed me for your sacrifices, but simply because I know what those sacrifices were and the toll they sometimes took on your physical, mental, and social well-being.

A friend once remarked to me after seeing you by my side, "Tony, you don't deserve someone as beautiful and wonderful as Lois." Amen! Thank God that He gives us what we don't deserve.

Finally, thank you, Lois, for making up for my deficiencies in the home. When I was traveling to tell others how to establish and develop their families, you were maintaining ours. When problems developed with the kids, especially during their transition into the teenage years, you made me take notice, slow down, and walk them through the crises. Even when I was wrong in my judgment, you kept me positioned as head of the family and never let the children divide us.

I know there are areas in your life that are not where you want them to be, and I know you have some personal goals you haven't yet accomplished. I want you to know that I am as committed to you as you have been to me, and I will live to let you know I'm honored to be able to call you my wife. You see, "Many daughters have done nobly, but you excel them all. Charm is deceitful and beauty is vain, but a woman who fears the Lord, she shall be praised. Give her the product of her hands, and let her works praise her in the gates" (Prov. 31:29-31). Lois, you are that woman, and it is my honor to give you that praise.

I treasure you deeply.

**Dear Chrystal; Priscilla;
Tony, Jr.; and Jonathan,**

The world in which you raise your own families will be a far cry from the world in which I grew up, and it will even be markedly different from the one you have come to know. As people continually remove themselves from God, we can only expect to see more and more of the kinds of devastation and cultural confusion that we have talked about so often in our family. I know that thought can be depressing, but in the midst of this badness, I have some good news for you. Just like you, Timothy received a godly heritage that would serve as a solid foundation for his life (see 2 Tim. 1:5), and he had to live in a world that got progressively worse (see 2 Tim. 3:1-7). So the apostle Paul's advice to him is the same I give to each of you: "You, however, continue in the things you have learned and become convinced of, knowing from whom you have learned them; and that from childhood you have known the sacred writings which are able to give you the wisdom that leads to salvation through faith which is in Christ Jesus. All scripture is inspired by God and profitable for teaching, reproof, for correction, for training in righteousness; that the man of God may be adequate, equipped for every good work" (2 Tim. 3:14-17).

Your mother and I have tried to instill in each of you God's truth that, if followed, can deliver you from the evils of this age as well as prepare you for the age to come. Only by following our Lord Jesus Christ and heeding His voice can you expect to find hope, peace, guidance, and strength for the uncertain days ahead.

Chrystal, my firstborn, I love you dearly. I remember well your growing-up years while I was going through seminary—how you used to hug me when I came home from class; how you refused to go to sleep unless we rocked you first. Even then you often refused to let us leave you. I also remember the groundings I had to give you because you went where you weren't supposed to go. Some of those teenage years were tumultuous. Well, you're all grown up now, and I'm proud of you. I'm proud every time I see you sing in the choir, and I'm proud when you tell me of the things you're learning. I pray for you when I hear of your struggles regarding your career plans.

God has given you a keen mind and sensitive spirit, but you also have a strong will. Please make sure that God always has freedom to bend and, when necessary, even break your will so that you're constantly being shaped in His image. Don't let Satan fool you with his buy now, pay later plan.

Don't let him make you satisfied with anything less than God's best for you.

Priscilla, Miss Personality, I love you as well. God has given you a unique ability to lead. Whether the area is academics, music, the church youth group, or athletics, you always seem to rise to the top.

Please use this special ability to lead others always in the path of righteousness and never down harm's way. Satan sees that ability and would like nothing more than to sift you like wheat so that he can use it to accomplish his purposes. That's why you must stay close to Christ. You must ask Him every step of the way whether or not this is what He would have you to do.

You say you want to sing. Well, my dear, sing to God's glory and to the encouragement of God's people. But remember: Minister, don't perform. Make sure your every note is sung for the Lord. Don't let the lure of power, prestige, money, or anything else take you away from the privilege of ministry. There is no better model for this than your own mother, who refuses to sing if she can't also minister.

Each time you sing at our church or radio rallies, my chest pops forward with pride at the powerful way you communicate God's truth in song. Always be conscious that both your voice and your personality are gifts from God that He wants back. Let Him have them so He can return them to you with power. "I urge you therefore, brethren, by the mercies of God, to present your bodies a living and holy sacrifice, acceptable to God, which is your spiritual service of worship. And do not be conformed to this world, but be transformed by the renewing of your mind, that you may prove what the will of God is, that which is good and acceptable and perfect" (Rom. 12:1-2).

Anthony, my beloved first son, I still chuckle when I think about the day you were born. After having two girls, I wanted a boy desperately when your mother went into the delivery room. I'll never forget the nurse coming into the waiting room. I had been sleeping, and she said, "Mr. Evans, it's a boy."

"A what!" I said.

"A boy."

"A what!"

"A boy!"

"Are you kidding?" I asked.

She assured me one more time that I had a son, and while I was cool on the outside, inside I was doing somersaults. I rushed to your mother's room, took one look at my firstborn son, and said his name is Anthony T. Evans, Jr.

Anthony, I'm proud of you and your love

for the Lord, your love for hurting people, and your willingness just to help, whether it's with the puppet ministry or youth council at church. I also enjoyed our time together at the pet store and riding horses. I gave you my name because I wanted to pass down to you my heritage. I want with all my heart for you to be a man after God's own heart. I want you to love Him with all your heart, mind, might, and soul.

Every time you're by my side, I stand proud that you're my son. Every time someone says, "That boy looks just like you," I stand taller, because you are my joy.

Son, wear that name with pride, not because there's something special in the name, but because there's someone special bearing the name. Always let that name reflect character so that others will respect you. Let that name reflect holiness so that God can always honor you. Let that name reflect dignity so that your own son will follow you.

I'm proud to give you my name, but I'm even prouder because you have committed yourself to Christ, and that means God has given you His name. "At the name of Jesus every knee shall bow ... and ... every tongue should confess that Jesus Christ is Lord, to the glory of God the Father" (Phil. 2:10-11).

Jonathan, my youngest, your name means

"a gift from God." Your mother picked that name because you were our little surprise from the Lord, and what a wonderful surprise you were. Your presence has brought great joy to our lives. I remember well how almost every night you climbed into our bed, sometimes ever so quietly so we wouldn't know you were there. I remember the hours we spent together working on homework or playing basketball.

God has given you a special sensitivity to spiritual things. Your mother and I will never forget the night you told us you wanted to accept Christ. The joy that filled our hearts and the tears that filled our eyes at the depth of your spiritual understanding at such a young age still astound us.

Never forget that you are indeed God's gift, not only to us but also to this world. You were uniquely created for a purpose. Find that purpose, and never leave it. God wants to use you to bring His gift of salvation to men and women, just as He gave it to you. "Whether, then, you eat or drink or whatever you do, do all to the glory of God" (1 Cor. 10:31).

Children, I don't know how long God will give us to you. I hope it's for a long time to come, but as you very well know, life is uncertain. Whatever time we have, however, your mother's and my commitment is to constantly give you a legacy that you can in turn transfer to our grandchildren. Our family alone will not be able to stem the tide of cultural decay that's engulfing us, but I want to make as big a dent as I can.

I know we didn't always respond as we should have. Sometimes we didn't fully understand all you were going through. Sometimes we should have listened more, while other times we should have corrected you more quickly. But one thing is certain: Any failure on our part was related to our human frailty, not our love. While our love was sometimes imperfect, it was always real.

Thank you, children, for helping your mother and father learn the meaning of family. You four will be the best judges of whether we've applied the principles in this book to our family. My prayer for all of us is that God in His grace will continuously bind us together with cords that cannot be broken, constantly nourishing us in His Word and giving us a heritage that will serve our posterity for generations to come, while also allowing the Evans clan to make a difference for the betterment of society at large and the building of God's kingdom. We love you unconditionally, and we will lift you before God's throne in prayer every day of our lives.

Maranatha

CHAPTER THIRTEEN

The House That God Built

A ll of us know the children's story "The Three Little Pigs." As the story goes, the big bad wolf wants to devour the three pigs at all costs. To protect themselves, the pigs constructed houses.

The first pig built his house of straw. The wolf descended upon it and demanded entrance. He said that if the pig didn't let him in, he would huff and puff and blow the house down, and that's exactly what he did.

His life threatened, the first pig ran to the house of his friend the second pig. The wolf tracked them down and uttered the same threat as before. While the wood house of the second pig was much stronger than that of the first pig, it was still no match for the power of the big bad wolf. Having been denied entrance, the wolf huffed and puffed and blew that house down as well.

The two pigs hurried to the home of pig number three. He had built his house of brick and was totally confident that no matter how violently the wolf huffed and puffed and blew on the outside, it was not going to affect him, because his house was solid as a rock. The wolf made numerous attacks on the house, but all to no avail. Why? The third pig's house had been constructed with the right kind of material.

Today there's a big bad wolf standing outside all our homes, seeking to blow them down. That wolf is called the world, and its attack is relentless. How well our families survive has everything to do with the kind of material we use to construct our houses. The lung power in the wolf of this world is so potent that it can destroy any family not made with God's building material.

In Genesis 18:19, God gave Abraham sound, clear instruction on how to construct a family that would stand. His word to Abraham sums up the message of this book: "For I have chosen him, in order that he may command his children and his household after him to keep the way of the Lord by doing righteousness and justice; in order that the Lord may bring upon Abraham what He has spoken about him."

Three things were necessary if Abraham

was to avoid the destruction of his home by the world. First, he was to give his family a sense of destiny, a sense of purpose that grew out of knowing his own purpose. Our world is full of meaningless distraction but very little purpose, and purposeless parents raise purposeless children. All great people have before them a sense of a destiny that transcends their own lives.

We need to see beyond our children to our grandchildren and even our great-grandchildren. We will have to begin looking at the world not simply for what it is, but also for what we wish it to become. Having determined what we want to see in the future generations of our families, we can then raise our children with a goal in mind rather than simply going through the motions for today.

An older man once asked me what I would like to have written on my tombstone when I die. I told him, "Tony Evans knew God and influenced the world for Him."

He then said, "Now that you know what you'd like said about you when you die, you'd better begin working on it today."

I never forgot that, because it gave me a sense of destiny. Even so for our children. What do you want them to look like when they're parents? You'd better start working on it now.

Second, God said of Abraham that he was

to discipline his children by commanding them in the way of the Lord. Notice that Abraham, the father, was to be the primary source of family discipline. This thought is also carried over into the New Testament when Paul told the church at Ephesus, "And fathers, do not provoke your children to anger, but bring them up in the discipline and instruction of the Lord" (Eph. 6:4).

The unruliness of this generation is directly attributable to either absent or spiritually impotent men in the home. Unless this trend is reversed, catastrophe awaits us. Abraham's authority in the disciplining process was both definitive and prescribed. He was to command his children, not suggest to them, and the basis of that authority was the Lord. He could not command them to do anything inconsistent with the Lord from whom he received his own commands. Parents today need to take a definitive role in commanding conformity from their children, but only as we trust and obey God.

One time I asked my son to take out the trash. He responded, "Dad, I don't feel like it."

Say what?! I thought. He was telling me that as my instructions hit his frontal lobe and were processed by his brain, and as the signal went down his spinal column through the various nerves that were to instruct the muscles to accomplish the task, there was not enough emotional stimulus to provoke his skeletal frame into a trash-emptying mode. To which I responded, "I can change the way you feel!"

In other words, he had to empty the trash for no other reason than I said so. (But by the same token, my son must not see me telling God, "I won't obey You because I don't feel like it.") Unless there is discipline to do right in the home, there will be little discipline to do right in society.

Finally, Abraham was to give his children dignity by teaching them righteousness and justice. The world is an unfair and insensitive place. Our children are born with that same tendency toward unfairness and insensitivity. That's why you don't have to teach them how to be selfish. No books are written on *The Ten Ways to Raise Evil Kids.* They manage to be self-centered all by themselves. Our job as parents is to show them what's right, not only for their own benefit, but also for the benefit of society at large. We desperately need an army of families who both care and do something about the cycle of injustice in the world.

People are discarded like worn dolls when they're deemed useless or unnecessary. As a result, the poor among us are the most vulnerable, since they have little with which to fight back. However, God's heart is with the poor, and the measure of a strong Christian family, church, or society is how it treats the most defenseless citizens.

I never want my children to forget that they're recipients of God's grace in many ways. I always want them to see themselves as servants to others, especially to hurting people and those children in urban America who have never had the privilege of living with a mother and father. The only way that can be assured is for us as a family to actively minister grace to others.

Each Christmas we identify a family from one of our sister churches and purchase gifts for each person. Lois and I provide the food and take it to them and share a time of prayer, worship, and giving. In addition, I keep my kids vitally involved with our church's outreach to those in need.

Recently, Priscilla and Tony, Jr., went with their youth group to help families whose homes had been flooded in another section of Dallas. When they entered one home, an older lady told them she had just gotten off her knees from asking God how she was going to eat since she had lost everything. That's when the kids came with the food. My children broke down in tears at the thought that God had used them as His means of answering prayer. They have heard many a sermon from me on our responsibility to minister to others, but no sermon in the world could have been more powerful than the one the Holy Spirit preached to them by using them as emissaries of His grace.

Lois and I also tell our kids stories of how things were for us growing up without very much and how, during my seminary years, we wondered on more than one occasion how we were going to make it. Even then, however, we agreed it was best for Lois to stay home with our preschool-aged children. Now, when we hear our younger daughter sing her gospel music; when we see our older son working in the church's puppet ministry or joyfully painting houses for the disadvantaged; when we hear our older daughter saying her highest ambition is to be a godly wife and mother; and when we hear our younger son say he wants to grow up to help me in the ministry, we know that decision was worth all the sacrifice.

We take our kids every summer to the block where I grew up. As they see the devastation and deterioration of that neighborhood, it becomes a prime reminder of how God had preserved their father and why I'm in the ministry trying to help my people rise above the disintegration engulfing black America.

I often sit with my children, too, to talk about their futures—what colleges they'd like to go to and what careers they would like to pursue. After they've expressed themselves, I always ask the following questions: "How will the kingdom of God be better off if God gives you what you desire? How will those less fortunate be better off?" I let them know emphatically that until they can answer those questions, they will never have purpose, nor will they have God's full blessing on their lives. "Only one life, 'twill soon be past;/ Only what's done for Christ will last."

Genesis 18:19 closes with the proviso that if Abraham was ever going to see God accomplish all that God wanted to do through him, it would happen through his investment in his family. The same is true today. If the block where you live is ever going to become a better block, your neighborhood a better neighborhood, your city a better city, our nation a better nation, and our world a better world, it will start with you and your family.

If it doesn't work for you, don't transport it. But if you can overcome the influence of the world in your house, then maybe, just maybe, you can make a difference outside your house as well.

I can't help thinking again of my own father in this regard. He gave me the foundation, through his discipline and his consistent Christian character, for all I am and do. God has built on that foundation, I believe, in blessing me with a large, dynamic church and an urban ministry that touches thousands of lives across the world.

God also gave me two special occasions on which I got to honor Dad publicly. One was when I introduced him to my congregation and told them my ministry to them was just an extension of his ministry to me. Then I heard them thank him for raising his son to be their pastor. The other was when our ministry, The Urban Alternative, received the Anschutz Family Foundation Award for our outreach to the black family.

I didn't feel my work could be honored legitimately without also honoring him, so I invited him and Mom to the ceremony in Washington, D.C. And as part of my acceptance speech, I described all he had done for me. Then I called him forward and presented a plaque I had ordered to express my gratitude on that special night.

Now that Anschutz award sits on my desk as a beautiful picture of what the family is supposed to be. It's a bronze statue of a family of eagles. The mother is perched on a mountain, with her eaglets tucked safely under her wings, while the father hovers above with his wings outstretched to protect and preserve his loved ones. What a powerful illustration of the Christian home!

We must never be content with simply protecting our kids from the world. Rather, our goal should be to equip them to help change the world so that when they go out into it, they do so as lights in the midst of darkness. If we do our parenting job right, and they choose to walk with God, it won't be them so much as the world that's in trouble because of the impact they'll make upon it.

Even if the society at large doesn't become a noticeably better place, however, you and your house will still be victorious. No one has summed up this truth any better than Joshua: "Now, therefore, fear the Lord and serve Him in sincerity and truth; and put away the gods which your fathers served beyond the River and in Egypt, and serve the Lord. And if it is disagreeable in your sight to serve the Lord, choose for yourselves today whom you will serve: whether the gods which your fathers served which were beyond the River, or the gods of the Amorites in whose land you are living; but as for me and my house, we will serve the Lord" (Josh. 24:14-15). What about your house?

A Message to My People

Nowhere is the demise of the family more obvious than in urban America in general and the black community in particular. The crisis in the culture at large has become a catastrophe among my people.

At one time, our community provided one of the best illustrations of biblical family life that our world has ever seen. Taking their cue from the Old Testament, black neighborhoods operated like extended families. Almost everyone you knew was like an aunt, uncle, or cousin. The elderly were treated with utmost respect, and everyone held everyone else accountable for proper behavior. Bearing and raising children was viewed as a great goal and privilege, and marriage was held in the highest esteem.

Most amazingly, all this took place in some

terribly inhumane environments. Yet in spite of slavery, Jim Crow, segregation, and discrimination, the black family was held together by an unshakable faith in God and a tenacious spirit rooted in hope. The church was the center of community life, bolstering the family and reinforcing hope, and the role models children needed lived next door or at worst a block away.

How times have changed! Today, half of all black children are being raised without a father in the home. While the teen pregnancy rate in our country is bad enough, in the black community it's beyond human comprehension—90 percent of all babies born to black teens are born to unwed mothers. When you add to that the economic tragedy (50 percent of all black children grow up in poverty), it's no wonder we're a people living on the edge.

Furthermore, consider that the number one cause of death for black young men is homicide; that black boys drop out of school in staggering numbers (70 percent in inner-city New York); and that more black men are in prison than in college (one of every four black males is involved in some aspect of the criminal justice system). The repercussions for the family are enormous. We now have a generation of women with no one to marry; five women for every available man. A recent conference at Howard University concluded that the only solution is for black women to share their men.

In days gone by, if the parents couldn't or wouldn't take care of their young, the grandparents would take them in. The children would thus receive the love and wisdom of their elderly grandparents. Today, however, Grandma is between thirty-five and forty years old and likely single herself, struggling to survive and without the time or experience to provide the wisdom her grandchildren need. That reality has left us with a generation that in many ways must raise itself.

The advent of drugs and gangs has provided a way for these directionless young people to meet their economic and social needs with one move. But the price to our community is measured in loss of life, hope, property, and family stability. Even the black middle class has succumbed to the society's diseases of divorce, abuse, and child neglect. We are indeed a community at risk.

A number of things must happen quickly if the black family is to be saved. First, our churches must reclaim their position as community leaders.

The church is the only institution that can save our people. There are several reasons this is true. First, it's the only institution owned and operated by our community nationwide.

Second, it's the only institution that has God's blessing for the express purpose of building the family, and it's called a family itself by the Lord.

Third, it's the only institution with access to all black people everywhere. There are about 65,000 black churches for the 9.6 million black families in the United States, or one church for every 148 households—more than enough to get the job done.

Fourth, it already has the people and skills needed to address the issues we face (more about that shortly).

Fifth, the church is the only institution that mobilizes massive numbers of black people every week in the same place.

Finally, the very purpose of the church is to provide the spiritual and moral fiber whose lack is the major cause of family breakdown. Without a church-led renewal of the historically high spiritual standards that once dominated our culture, we are doomed.

For the first time in our history, we have a generation of kids with no spiritual hooks. We always used to have something or someone we could count on to call our children back to what's right—a grandparent, teacher, neighbor, or community or church leader who reflected a divine perspective on life. But today, the children of urban America have few such links left, and without them, we have no means of snatching the children from the moral quicksand rapidly engulfing them. Only an aggressive, radical, spiritually based outreach will save them from destruction.

Specifically, the black church must start doing three things immediately in addition to what's already been said in this book. First, more of our pastors must teach God's Word from the pulpit. We have no time for nice stories, social theories, and political rhetoric. We need divine authority and biblically based answers. Pastors hold the key, as they always have in our community.

Second, we must begin to hold people accountable for their lifestyles. Currently, people can worship one way on Sunday (or not worship at all) and live another way on Monday, and no one calls them to task. Everyone, from our leaders to our children, *must* be held accountable. Everyone should know that the church will not tolerate immoral living, drunkenness, cheating, discrimination, or any other rebellious activity. Deacons must be deacons, deputized to oversee the implementation of God's Word in the life of the church.

Finally, the church must operate as a comprehensive ministry. We must not only win people to Christ for heaven, but also show them how to change their status in history. Here again the church is key, because in the urban community, it is uniquely equipped to assist families in every dimension of life.

Many churches don't realize they already have the resources in place to accomplish their task. Every member is a potential staff member when it comes to expertise. Every need the family has can usually be met by someone else sitting in the pew. The problem is that many church members don't understand it's their job to do the work of the ministries. Doctors are supposed to doctor for the kingdom. Typists are typists for the kingdom. School teachers are teachers for the kingdom.

The mission of every church, then, should be to mobilize its members to use their skills in Christian ministry. Like no other group in America, we have both the ability and the historical experience to demonstrate to the culture at large how to save a generation. That's because the black church knows how to infuse God into every institution in society, whether it be the schools, legal system, or businesses.

Our challenge is to stop giving excuses for why we *can't* change things and start determining how we *will* change things. We don't have a resource problem. Nor are we deficient in the necessary skills. If all members of our churches began to use their abilities under the authority of Scripture, all our family needs would be met through the church. The solutions to our problems are asleep in our pews.

One of the most important things the urban church can do is to empower families economically. For example, a church can develop a job-training and skill-development ministry that helps members and others in the community to become employable. Skills such as data processing, computer programming, and light bookkeeping, to name just a few, are all fairly easily transferable. When translated into jobs, such skills help people to help themselves and their families, which in turn makes them less dependent on the government and the church. At our church in Dallas, we teach all the above in our Social Service Center.

The church can also provide educational assistance by becoming a certified GED center and training those who have yet to complete high school. And many colleges today are looking for community-based organizations that can serve as off-site campuses.

Churches that really want to take the bull by the horns can develop complete businesses so that they have a mechanism for generating capital while at the same time providing jobs for members. Churches can also offer a job referral center where those in need of employment can be matched with employers both inside and outside the church.

The exciting thing about such referrals is that the church, unlike any other employment agency, can provide additional accountability to the employer on how well the employee functions. As we come to the turn of the century with a shrinking labor force, it's increasingly important to employers that they get reliable workers. What better place to get them than the church?

The beauty of all the above suggestions is that almost all of them can be developed and directed by people in the church. The key is getting members to see that their God-given abilities are meant for more than just generating personal income. God has equipped them for promoting His kingdom, and what better investment of time and energy can there be than helping families become financially stable by equipping them to take care of their own?

A New Attitude

If the urban family is to be rebuilt, however, it must also change its attitude. Rather than spending so much time talking about how bad things are, we must begin to look for and operate out of our own strengths. That means we must stop depending on government to do for us what we're responsible to do for ourselves. To be sure, we must use our rights as citizens to change those things that hurt our families. But complaining about who's in the White House and what government grants have been rejected won't put food on our tables, men in our homes, and roofs over our heads. Those are our responsibilities, and we have the financial wherewithal to meet them.

The gross national product of black America is quickly approaching $300 billion a year, which, if we were an independent nation, would make us the ninth largest in the world economically. So we can do what we will to do in spite of the negative circumstances surrounding us.

Racism is real and evil. It must be resisted and ultimately defeated. But complaining about racism is only valid insofar as it reveals what we're up against. It's no more valid an excuse not to function properly as families as it would be for the Dallas Cowboys to complain that they can't move forward because eleven other men keep getting in the way. The idea is to show how strong you are by going through, around, or over the opposition.

Furthermore, racism has absolutely nothing to do with some of the things it gets blamed for. Racism is not responsible for producing babies out of wedlock; illegitimate sex is. Nor is racism responsible for aborting those babies once they've been conceived. Racism isn't responsible for black-on-black crime; it doesn't pull the trigger. Racism doesn't keep our kids in front of the TV instead of the textbook. Racism doesn't make a man leave his family, and it doesn't stop the black middle class from reaching back to help those less fortunate.

Admittedly, racism may create a climate where some of those evils flourish more easily, but we must never succumb to its influence. It has been around a long time, and it doesn't seem it will disappear in the near future. So while it ought to be addressed and fought, it cannot be allowed to keep us from doing what needs to be done. *We should determine what our families would look like if racism didn't exist and then go about building such families.*

My parents didn't have access to a lot of family seminars and the newest Christian literature while my siblings and I were growing up; in those years, blacks were rarely included in major Christian outreaches. But they did have the Bible and a passionate love for Jesus Christ, each other, and their children—and somehow that was enough. That's sufficient proof for me that economic, racial, and class limitations need not be the last word in how children turn out.

We black parents must also take responsibility for our own children. We must stop depending on other groups to raise, educate, and serve as role models for our kids. That's not to say that others can't come alongside and provide assistance and encouragement. But it is to say that the onus is on us to raise our children properly.

We have to see to it that the TV is turned off and our kids get into the books. We have to monitor their friendships and acquaintances. We have to teach them a solid work ethic and an appreciation for their history. We have to provide the strong surrogate male Christian models they so desperately need. We have to teach them how to save, spend, and give.

Most important of all, we have to give our children the moral and spiritual foundation with which they can—and will want to—reject the negative values thrust upon them. That means first and foremost that we have to begin taking ourselves and our kids to church—Bible-teaching, Christ-centered, culturally relevant churches. Unless we demonstrate the importance of church in the life of the family, our kids won't learn it.

Likewise, unless we exemplify the kind of values we wish our children to possess, why should they accept them? Why should they reject the get-rich-quick schemes of the drug pusher if there are no parents teaching them the dignity of honorable work? Why should our teenage girls stop getting pregnant if they feel the only way they can receive unconditional love is through the birth of their own babies? Why should our boys stop dropping out of high school when no one is holding them accountable for doing their homework and few parents are attending the parent-teacher meetings to see how their children are doing? Why should our kids avoid gangs if there is no home environment providing acceptance, recognition, dignity, and esteem? Why should our kids not disrespect their elders when parents don't insist on respect and when kids see their parents disrespecting each other? Why should the children of middle-class black families take the time to care for the less-fortunate in our communities if their parents are too busy to be concerned for the family and friends they left behind?

To be sure, many parents in urban America are doing a wonderful job in guiding their children through this misguided world. But many more of us have to start doing this job if we're to save our communities. If they could, our grandparents would rise out of their graves and spank us as a people for the way we've allowed the negative conditions we face to wreak havoc in our homes—especially since they suffered and sacrificed so much to secure the survival of our families.

Our world has become so terribly misguided that we can't look to it to help us do the job God entrusted to the family: raise children who can change the direction of our communities because they have been taught to march to a different drumbeat. We the parents will have to create that new sound, and our churches must teach us how to play the tune, using the Bible as our instruction manual.

The time has come for a revival in the black family—for a "new generation" of parents full of hope, strength, commitment, and God's Word. We need men to become men rather than simply wanting to be leaders— men who put the interests of their wives and children above their own; who have the guts to take a stand against the lawlessness of our day; who reject immorality as their right and privilege and understand that women are not tools for their gratification but wonderful creations of God, given to help men become all they were meant to be. We need to reject the lie that real men are like Rambo or Dirty Harry and raise real men who, like Jesus, are people of integrity, dignity, strength, love, sensitivity, and absolute standards.

We also need women who understand

they are too valuable to be misused by undisciplined males—women who count their virginity as an honor until they get married and understand that their job is to take all the skills and gifts God has given them and direct them toward the common good of the home. We need women who respect their husbands as head of the home in the same way they respect their bosses at work; they don't always agree with them, but they honor their position. We need women like Sarah, who did not consider it belittling to call Abraham "lord" (though we don't use such words today) because she understood that men need the support of their wives if they're going to see the fulfillment of God's promises for their homes.

If we're to save our families, we're going to have to stop running sprints as a people and start running marathons. Anyone can sprint, but you have to be well-conditioned to run a marathon. We need parents who have become spiritually disciplined enough to make their personal gratification secondary to the well-being of their children; to study, listen, and learn from those resources that can help them do a better job of parenting; to get on their knees and ask God to guard and guide their children; to live exemplary lives before them.

We are too great a people with too great a

God and too rich a heritage to have the kind of family disintegration we're now experiencing. It will take every ounce of our energy to reclaim our families. But if not now, when? And if not us, who?

Notes

Chapter 1
1. Joseph Farah, "TV's Assault on Families Is No Joke," *Focus on the Family*, Nov. 1990, p. 10.
2. Ibid., p. 11.
3. Josh McDowell, *Why Wait?* (San Bernardino, Cal.: Here's Life, 1987), p. 40.
4. Farah, "TV's Assault," p. 11.
5. From a Texas Instruments ad in *Newsweek*, Oct. 1, 1990, p. 1.
6. McDowell, *Why Wait?*, p. 40.
7. James C. Dobson, "The Second Great Civil War," *Focus on the Family*, Nov. 1990, p. 3.

Chapter 2
1. "Shameful Bequests to the Next Generation," *Time*, Oct. 8, 1990, p. 45.

Chapter 3
1. Ross Campbell, *How to Really Love Your Child* (Wheaton, Ill.: Victor, 1977), p. 32.
2. M. Scott Peck, *The Road Less Traveled* (New York: Touchstone, 1978), p. 81.

Chapter 5
1. Bill Gaither, "A Few Good Men," *Christian Herald*, Nov./Dec. 1990, p. 19.

Chapter 6

1. Donald E. Sloat, *The Dangers of Growing Up in a Christian Home* (Nashville: Nelson, 1986), pp. 26-27.
2. Ibid., pp. 154-55.

Chapter 7

1. Tipper Gore, *Raising PG Kids in an X-Rated Society* (Nashville: Abingdon, 1987), p. 12.
2. Quoted by Rolf Zettersten with Jim Ware, "In Focus," *Focus on the Family*, Oct. 1989, p. 15.

Chapter 10

1. Jean Kilbourne, "Deadly Persuasion," *Adolescent Counselor,* Nov./Dec. 1990, p. 5.
2. Ibid.
3. Ibid.
4. James C. Dobson, *Dr. Dobson Answers Your Questions about Raising Children* (Wheaton, Ill.: Tyndale, 1982), p. 218.
5. James C. Dobson and Gary L. Bauer, *Children at Risk* (Dallas: Word, 1990), p. 52.
6. Dobson, *Dr. Dobson Answers Your Questions*, p. 86.

A Personal Word

The blessing of writing this book is that it has forced me to examine carefully my own strengths and weaknesses as a husband and father. The more I wrote, the more convicted I became of my shortcomings. The good news, however, is that I've also been reenergized in my commitment to guide my family through this misguided world. I've already decided on some changes I'll make immediately to give my wife and children the time, attention, and love they need and deserve. I'm going to stop making them wait until tomorrow. Tomorrow is now. So thank you for helping me.

My prayer is that God has also used this book to encourage, challenge, and strengthen you to make a difference in the world through your own family. Only as families are built and rebuilt according to God's original design can we ever hope to see our world steered in the right direction.

If by chance you've read this far and you're not yet a Christian, I implore you to give your life to Jesus Christ as your personal Savior today. He loves you and gave His life on the cross in your place, for your sins. His resurrection proved that He is indeed the Son of God and that He accomplished His divine purpose. When you place your faith in Christ alone as your means of forgiveness from sin, God will spiritually start your life over by changing you from the inside out and then enabling you to reach others, beginning with your own family.

If you've made a new commitment as a result of reading this book, if you would simply like to express what the book has meant to you, or if you'd like more information about the conference, tape, and printed resources of The Urban Alternative (TUA), please write me at:

The Urban Alternative
P. O. Box 4000
Dallas, TX 75208

Our goal at TUA is to help rebuild families by equipping churches to reach out and minister effectively in their own communities. Please pray for us as we take our message throughout America.

May God bless you as you and your biblically guided family shine bright in our misguided world.

Dr. Anthony T. Evans

Other Books to Strengthen Your Relationships
From Focus on the Family®

Parents Guide to Top 10 Dangers Teens Face
Parents can help guard their teens against alcoholism, drug addiction, promiscuity, and other reckless behaviors by reading Stephen Arterburn's Parents Guide to Top 10 Dangers Teens Face. Filled with proven principles, it helps parents heed the warning signs, ward off potential problems, and direct their kids down the road to success. Paperback.

Give Them Wings
When kids hit their teenage years, the role of parents begins to change. In Give Them Wings, author Carol Kuykendall offers encouragement for raising kids to be responsible, godly men and women and for looking toward the empty nest with hope. Paperback.

Once a Parent, Always a Parent
Kids grow up, but they're still your kids! Steven Bly in Once a Parent, Always a Parent shares practical ways to become involved—but not over-involved— in your adult child's life. Learn how to best provide support, encouragement, financial assistance, childcare, and much more whether your child lives across the country or across the hall. Paperback.

Look for these special books in your Christian bookstore or request a copy by calling 1-800-A-FAMILY (1-800-232-6459). Friends in Canada may write Focus on the Family, P.O. Box 9800, Stn. Terminal, Vancouver, B.C. V6B 4G3 or call 1-800-661-9800.

Visit our Web site (www.family.org) to learn more about the ministry or to find out if there is a Focus on the Family office in your country.

9BPXMP

FOCUS ON THE FAMILY.
Welcome to the Family!

Whether you received this book as a gift, borrowed it from
a friend, or purchased it yourself, we're glad you read it!
It's just one of the many helpful, insightful, and encouraging
resources produced by Focus on the Family.

In fact, that's what Focus on the Family is all about—
providing inspiration, information, and biblically based
advice to people in all stages of life.

It began in 1977 with the vision of one man, Dr. James Dobson,
a licensed psychologist and author of 16 best-selling books on
marriage, parenting, and family. Alarmed by the societal, political,
and economic pressures that were threatening the existence
of the American family, Dr. Dobson founded Focus on the Family
with one employee—an assistant—and a once-a-week
radio broadcast, aired on only 36 stations.

Now an international organization, Focus on the Family is
dedicated to preserving Judeo-Christian values and strengthening
the family through more than 70 different ministries, including
eight separate daily radio broadcasts; television public service
announcements; 11 publications; and a steady series of
award-winning books, films, and videos for people
of all ages and interests.

Recognizing the needs of, as well as the sacrifices and important
contribution made by, such diverse groups as educators, physi-
cians, attorneys, crisis pregnancy center staff, and single parents,
Focus on the Family offers specific outreaches to uphold and minister to these individuals, too. And it's all done for one purpose,
and one purpose only: to encourage and strengthen individuals
and families through the life-changing message of Jesus Christ.

• • •

For more information about the ministry, or if we can be of help to
your family, simply write to Focus on the Family, Colorado Springs,
CO 80995 or call 1-800-A-FAMILY (1-800-232-6459). Friends in
Canada may write Focus on the Family, P.O. Box 9800, Stn.
Terminal, Vancouver, B.C. V6B 4G3 or call 1-800-661-9800. Visit our
Web site—www.family.org—to learn more about the ministry or to
find out if there is a Focus on the Family office in your country.

We'd love to hear from you!